The Speech Therapist's Guide to
Autism Parenting

Practical Strategies to Reduce Meltdowns, Improve Communication, Manage Daily Routines, and Support Your Child's Growth with Confidence

Kids SLT Publications

© **Copyright 2025 by Kids SLT Publications - All rights reserved.**

The content contained within this book may not be reproduced, duplicated, or transmitted without direct written permission from the author or the publisher. Under no circumstances will any blame or legal responsibility be held against the publisher or author for any damages, reparation, or monetary loss due to the information contained within this book, either directly or indirectly.

Legal Notice:

This book is copyright-protected. It is only for personal use. You cannot amend, distribute, sell, use, quote or paraphrase any part or the content within this book, without the consent of the author or publisher.

Disclaimer Notice:

Please note that the information contained within this document is for educational purposes only. All effort has been made to present accurate, up-to-date, and reliable, complete information. No warranties of any kind are declared or implied. Readers acknowledge that the author is not engaging in the rendering of legal, Financial, medical, or professional advice.

The content within this book has been derived from various sources. Please consult a licensed professional before attempting any techniques outlined in this book. By reading this document, the reader agrees that under no circumstances is the author responsible for any losses, direct or indirect, which are incurred as a result of the use of the information contained within this document, including but not limited to errors, omissions, or inaccuracies

Table of Contents

Introduction 9

Chapter 1 Understanding Autism, Foundations For Empowered Parenting 13

    Spotting Early Signs—Milestones, Red Flags, And When To Seek Assessment 13

    Social, Language, And Behavioral Red Flags 14

    The Spectrum Explained—Traits, Variations, And Co-Occurring Conditions 15

    Neurodiversity In Action—Why Autism Is A Difference, Not A Deficit 18

    Debunking Myths—Separating Fact From Fiction About Autism 20

    Building "My Child's Profile"—Tracking Strengths, Triggers, And Preferences 22

    Sample "All About Me" Worksheet 23

    Navigating The Diagnosis Journey—Scripts, Questions, And Action Steps 25

Chapter 2: Creating Connection—Strengthening Bonds Through Responsive Communication 29

    Tuning In—Reading Your Child's Signals And Nonverbal Cues. 29

    Try This: Communication Pattern Tracker 31

    The Power Of Play—Connection Before Correction 31

    Responsive Communication—Mirroring, Modeling, And Wait Time 33

Scripting And Echolalia—Harnessing Repetition For Understanding 35

Recognizing Patterns And Building Bridges 36

Expanding Scripted Language.. 36

Supporting Flexibility And Growth 37

Responding Supportively 37

Navigating Scripting In Social Settings 37

Building Trust During Meltdowns—Co-Regulation Techniques. 38

Using Social Stories—Preparing For Change And New Experiences.. 40

Chapter 3: Communication For All—Tools, Tech, And Strategies To Support Every Child... 43

Choosing The Right Communication Tools—AAC, PECS, And More 43

Interactive Element: Decision Flowchart For Communication Supports 45

Introducing Visual Supports—Schedules, Choice Boards, And Timers 46

Low-Tech Communication Hacks—Everyday Items For Big Impact 48

Making AAC Routine—Integrating Devices At Home And School 50

Troubleshooting Communication Frustrations—Common Roadblocks And Fixes... 52

Practical Exercise: Reflection Prompt..................................... 54

Supporting Siblings As Communication Partners................... 54

- Chapter 4: Calming The Storm—Meltdown Management And Emotional Regulation 57
  - Understanding Meltdowns Vs. Tantrums—What's Really Happening? 57
  - Visual Comparison Chart: Meltdowns Vs. Tantrums 58
  - Sensory Triggers—Building A Personalized Sensory Profile 59
  - Sensory Diary Template 61
  - The Calming Toolkit—Weighted Items, Fidgets, And Sensory Diets 62
  - Weighted Items 63
  - Fidgets, Chewelry, And Headphones 63
  - Keeping The Toolkit Dynamic 63
  - The Sensory Diet: Regulation Throughout The Day 64
  - Public Meltdowns—Quick-Reference Flowcharts For Crisis Moments 64
  - Quick-Reference Flowchart: Before, During, After 65
  - Before Meltdown: 65
  - During Meltdown: 65
  - After Meltdown: 65
  - After The Storm—Repairing Connection And Rebuilding Safety 66
  - Preventing Overwhelm—Micro-Routines And Transition Strategies 69
- Chapter 5: Daily Life, Simplified—Building Routines That Work For Your Family 73
  - Morning Routines—Visual Schedules And "First-Then" Boards 73

Visual Routine Builder—Quick Exercise 74

Mealtime Solutions—Handling Picky Eating And Food Aversions 75

Sleep Support—Creating Calm Evenings And Predictable Bedtimes 77

Bedtime Routine Reflection 79

Getting Out The Door—Transition Routines For School And Outings 79

Chore Time—Teaching Life Skills Through Play And Predictability 81

Adapting For Sensory Needs—Home Setups That Reduce Stress 84

Chapter 6: Advocacy And Access—Navigating Schools, Therapies, And Community Life 87

Navigating The IEP Process—Scripts, Checklists, And Red Flags 87

IEP Milestone Checklist 88

Reflection Exercise: Your Parent Input Statement 89

Communicating With Teachers—Templates For Effective Home-School Notes 89

Choosing Therapies—Speech, OT, DIR/Floor Time, And Evidence-Based Alternatives 92

Decision Worksheet: Is This Therapy A Good Fit? 93

Understanding ABA—Controversies, Consent, And Parent Decision-Making 94

Accessing Funding And Community Resources—Grants, Medicaid, NHS, And More 97

Handling Pushback—Advocating When Family Or School Doesn't "Get It" 100

Advocacy Log Template 102

Chapter 7: Family, Friends, And The Wider World—Strengthening Your Support Network 103

Supporting Siblings—Age-Appropriate Explanations And Activities 103

Reflection Exercise: Sibling Connection Journal 105

Building Inclusive Family Rituals—Everyone Belongs 105

Explaining Autism To Extended Family And Friends—Scripts And Story Cards 107

Social Skills In Real Life—Playdates, Community Events, And Clubs 109

Handling Stares And Judgment—Comebacks And Coping Strategies 112

Finding Your Village—Support Groups, Online Communities, And Peer Mentors 114

Chapter 8: Hope, Growth, And Self-Care—Sustaining Your Journey Together 117

Preventing Burnout—Five-Minute Self-Care Routines For Busy Parents 117

Interactive Element: Five-Minute Self-Care Menu 118

Managing Guilt And Comparison—Reframing Progress And Success 119

Celebrating Bright Spots—Milestone Logs And Strengths-Based Journaling 121

Weekly Milestone Log Template 123

Planning For The Future—Transition Skills And Future Files.. 123

Promoting Self-Advocacy—Empowering Your Child's Voice ... 125

Staying Current—Building Your Personalized Resource Toolkit 128

Visual Element: Sample Google Drive "Autism Toolkit" Structure 130

A Humble Request! 131

Conclusion 133

References 137

Introduction

The clock ticks past midnight. A mother sits at her kitchen table. Papers from the clinic are spread out in front of her. Her child is finally asleep after a day filled with tears, meltdowns, and a constant struggle to find a way to communicate. The diagnosis is new. Autism. Her mind races with questions. What does this mean for my child? For our family? She feels a mix of hope, fear, confusion, and fierce love all at once. At that moment, she wants more than anything to help her child, but does not know where to start.

If you recognize yourself in this scene, you are not alone. I have met countless parents at this very crossroads, full of love and worry, looking for answers and support. I am a speech and language therapist with over twenty years of experience working with autistic children and their families. I have sat in living rooms, classrooms, and therapy rooms with thousands of families. I listened to their struggles and celebrated their triumphs. My commitment is to walk beside families through both the hard days and the hopeful ones.

Receiving a diagnosis or even suspecting autism can shake the ground beneath your feet. You may be feeling overwhelmed, confused, or even isolated. Perhaps you're unsure about what to do next. Maybe you are searching for a way to help your child thrive in a world that does not always understand or accommodate their needs. These feelings are common, and you are not alone in them. I want you to know that support is possible, and you have a partner in this book.

This guide is intended to serve as a lifeline. It is filled with practical strategies you can use today, not just theories or generic advice. The ideas here are drawn from research and from real families, families who have faced the same storms you are facing now. Every chapter offers tools and stories that are tried, tested, and rooted in real life. You will not find quick fixes or pressure to change your child into someone they are not. Instead, you will find ways to strengthen your connection, build new skills, and create a home where your child can grow with confidence.

What sets this book apart is its commitment to evidence-based, strengths-focused, and neurodiversity-affirming approaches. I do not offer outdated "fix-it" models. You will not find the rigid, one-size-fits-all systems that ignore the individuality of your child. While Applied Behavior Analysis (ABA) is sometimes mentioned as a therapy option, I only address it briefly and acknowledge the controversy it faces, especially within the UK autism community. My goal is to honor the voices of autistic people and their families and to support you in making decisions that feel right for your child.

Here is what you can expect as you read. We will discuss how to recognize early signs and understand common challenges, such as meltdowns, difficulty with changes, and communication breakdowns. You will learn how to reduce the overwhelm by setting realistic expectations and simplifying your routines. I will share ways to build strong bonds with your child through responsive communication, play, and everyday moments. There are chapters on supporting language with visual supports, modeling, and interactive games. You will find guidance on teaching independence, from basic life skills to daily choices, all through gentle support and clear routines.

We will also explore how to create routines that align with your child's sensory needs and your family's lifestyle. You will read stories from parents who have walked this path, stories of setbacks, breakthroughs, and the small joys that can shine even on hard days. You will find checklists, scripts, and customizable tools to help you advocate for your child in school, in therapy, and within your own extended family. And because your well-being matters too, we will discuss caring for yourself, building a supportive community, and maintaining hope for the long term.

This book is for every parent who is raising, or suspects they may be raising, an autistic child. It is for families of all shapes and sizes, from every background and community. Whether your child is speaking or non-speaking, newly diagnosed or older, this guide is for you. The tools and strategies are flexible so that you can adapt them for your child's age, abilities, and unique needs. There is no single "right" way, only the way that works for your child and your family.

You will find no judgment here. You will find encouragement, understanding, and practical help. I hope that you will use this book as a toolkit and a companion, returning to it whenever you need ideas or reassurance. With each page, I want you to feel seen, supported, and inspired to keep going.

Growth is possible. Every family's journey will look different, and that is not just okay, it is wonderful. The challenges are real, but so are the moments of connection, laughter, and progress. With the right tools and mindset, your child can flourish. So can you. Let us walk this path together, with courage and hope, and watch as your family discovers new strengths and joys along the way.

Chapter 1
Understanding Autism, Foundations for Empowered Parenting

I recall a father in my office, desperate yet fearful, clutching questions about his son's behaviors, lining up cars, not responding to his name, and melting down over changes. He wanted clarity, unsure if these quirks were typical or signs of something more serious. Parents in similar situations often seek answers, wanting to spot what matters without panicking or overlooking something important. This chapter is for you; to bring clarity and help you confidently consider the next steps.

Spotting Early Signs—Milestones, Red Flags, and When to Seek Assessment

Children develop at their own pace, but some differences persist and are notable. You might see your child doesn't follow your gaze, rarely waves, says only a few words by eighteen months, or prefers spinning wheels over showing toys. Signs can also be subtle, a toddler playing alone, lining up objects for a long time, avoiding eye contact, or reacting strongly to sounds. These quirks might be typical, but sometimes they suggest something to watch more closely.

Development is diverse. Some late talkers quickly catch up; some shy kids open up at home. What distinguishes early autism is the consistency of certain patterns, particularly in communication, play, and social interactions. Most twelve-month-olds look up when you say their name. If yours does not, even after multiple tries, it's notable. By eighteen months, most toddlers point to show you things. Lack of pointing or sharing objects is another sign. At two, pretend play, such as feeding a teddy or zooming cars, usually flourishes. If it doesn't, or if play is repetitive (such as spinning or lining up toys), it may be worth closer attention.

Here's a practical checklist for parents and caregivers. These signs alone do not diagnose autism but can guide your observations and discussions with professionals.

Social, Language, and Behavioral Red Flags

12 months:
- No response to name
- Rare smiles
- Limited eye contact
- No gestures like waving

18 months:
- No single words
- Rarely points or shows objects
- Disinterest in social games (peekaboo)
- Repeated actions

24 months:
- No two-word phrases (beyond echoing)
- Loss of previously acquired skills
- Little interest in peers
- Unusual sensitivity to sounds, textures, lights

Remember, many children have quirks; lining up crayons or repeating bedtime rituals doesn't mean autism. It's the persistence of these patterns and their impact on daily life that matters. For example, a child who lines up toys but still interacts and plays pretend is likely just quirky; a child who does it for long stretches, resists interruption, and avoids others may need evaluation.

If you're concerned, start tracking what you notice. Use a phone or notebook and consider recording brief video clips showing both strengths and challenges. Milestone trackers from your pediatrician or reputable websites can help. Provide specific examples rather than general feelings when discussing with professionals.

Bring your notes and videos to your pediatrician or early intervention team. Clearly share your concerns and examples from daily life. For instance, say, "My daughter rarely looks when I call her name and doesn't point to show me things. I'm worried she isn't using words like her peers." If your concerns are dismissed but your instincts persist, consider asking for an autism-specific screening tool, such as the M-CHAT-R, or request a specialist referral.

Early identification is crucial because support can truly make a difference. There's no need to panic at the first red flag. Some children catch up over time or with support. Trust your instincts and give yourself room to breathe.

Early signs of autism are not always obvious and can differ from child to child. Some children play differently, preferring objects over people or choosing solitary play. Others react strongly to certain sensory experiences, covering their ears, fixating on spinning fans, or avoiding messy textures. These tendencies often emerge only when looking back or comparing them to typical milestones.

Most important is noticing patterns that persist and impact daily life, not overanalyzing every quirk but paying close attention when something consistent feels different. By recognizing these signs early and seeking guidance, you give your child the best chance to grow with support tailored to their needs.

The Spectrum Explained—Traits, Variations, and Co-occurring Conditions

Imagine a row of paint swatches stretching across a wall. Each square is a different shade, some bright, some muted, some with flecks of unexpected color. That's autism. It's not a single path or a linear scale; it's a spectrum, full of variety, with everyone's experience colored a little differently. Some children may speak in complete sentences before the age of two but struggle to engage in pretend play or join group games. Others might barely speak at all but show an incredible memory for facts about trains or dinosaurs. This unevenness is what we refer to as a "spiky profile." If you drew your child's skills on a chart, you'd see peaks and valleys, maybe high language skills but struggles with transitions, or excel at puzzles but get overwhelmed by noise in the grocery store. There isn't a straight line or one-size-fits-all description. Instead, every child brings a unique shape to their own chart.

Autism's core traits show up in social communication, patterns of behavior, and sensory processing. Social communication differences can be subtle or noticeable. Some kids rarely look others in the eye, while others glance up occasionally but find it uncomfortable to do so. You may notice your child doesn't point at distant objects or bring you toys to share excitement, which is called "joint attention." Instead of showing you the bird outside the window, they might watch it alone. Conversation can feel one-sided or repetitive. Your child may echo phrases from cartoons ("scripting") or talk endlessly about a favorite subject without noticing if others are listening.

Behavioral patterns often include rigidity and deep interests. A child might insist on wearing the same shirt every day or follow a strict bedtime ritual. If plans change unexpectedly, they could become upset, anxious, or even have a meltdown. Special interests, sometimes referred to as "spins" or "hyperfixations," can be intense and joyful. A five-year-old might memorize every car model or recite train schedules from memory. Repetitive movements, called "stims," like hand-flapping, rocking, or spinning objects, serve as soothing tools for many autistic people.

Sensory differences are another key part of the spectrum. Some children react strongly to sounds most of us barely notice: a flushing toilet, the hum of fluorescent lights, the vacuum cleaner. Others may seek out deep pressure (hugging tight objects), craving movement (spinning in circles), or become fascinated by visual patterns, such as sunlight flickering through leaves. Sensory sensitivities can swing both ways:

some kids are hypersensitive and avoid certain textures or sounds, while others are hyposensitive and seem unaware of pain or cold.

Autism rarely travels alone. It often comes with other conditions that can shape your child's strengths and challenges. Attention-Deficit/Hyperactivity Disorder (ADHD) frequently overlaps, making it hard for some kids to focus or sit still. Anxiety is common, too; unpredictability or social demands can trigger intense worry. Some children have epilepsy, which means seizures may be part of their daily reality. Others face gastrointestinal issues like chronic constipation or reflux. Sometimes, these physical problems affect sleep and mood as much as any communication challenge.

You may hear people describe autistic children as "high-functioning" or "low-functioning." These labels miss the mark and can do more harm than good. Functioning labels overlook the complexity of support needs and fail to recognize how strengths in one area can mask struggles in another. A child who speaks fluently may still require significant support with daily routines or managing sensory overload. Another child who is non-verbal might be able to solve advanced puzzles but require assistance with tasks such as dressing or eating safely. Instead of sorting children into boxes, professionals now focus on describing support needs and recognizing that these needs can change over time and across environments.

A real-life example: In my work with families, I met a bright six-year-old who could read chapter books far above her grade level but panicked each morning at the sound of the school bell. Her teachers saw her as having "high-functioning" reading skills but missed how much support she needed for transitions and sensory sensitivities. Her parents, meanwhile, felt torn between pride in her brilliance and worry over her daily distress. Once her support team mapped out her "spiky profile," they could celebrate her strengths while building tools to support her through her hardest moments.

Suppose you find yourself confused by the variety of experiences you hear about autism, one child talking early but struggling with friends. In that case, another who does not speak at all but connects through music, you're seeing the true nature of the spectrum. The key is understanding your child's unique pattern: where their peaks soar high, where valleys need gentle support, and how co-occurring conditions shape the overall landscape. This perspective shifts focus from labels to real life, helping you advocate for what your child genuinely needs each day.

Neurodiversity in Action—Why Autism Is a Difference, Not a Deficit

Neurodiversity means brains come in many forms. It's a word you'll hear more and more, especially from autistic adults and advocates. In simple terms, neurodiversity suggests that differences such as autism, ADHD, and dyslexia are natural variations, like being left- or right-handed, or having brown eyes instead of blue. It challenges the old idea that autistic traits are just problems to be fixed. Instead, it highlights that there are many ways to think, learn, and see the world. This view isn't just a feel-good slogan; it's grounded in research and personal experience. Autistic people themselves have driven this movement, pushing back against models that focus only on what's "wrong." They speak up for acceptance and real support, not for changing who they are at the core. When you look at your child through this lens, you see a whole person, not a checklist of deficits, but a unique individual with both struggles and gifts.

You may notice that your child's honesty, sometimes blunt, is always genuine. Many autistic children have a laser-sharp focus when they are passionate about something, spending hours memorizing details about dinosaurs, outer space, or train schedules. Their memory for facts or routines can be astonishing. Some subtle patterns that most adults miss include spotting tiny changes in their environment or hearing rhythms in background noise. Creativity often manifests in surprising ways, perhaps through building intricate structures out of blocks or inventing new rules for games. Loyalty and fairness tend to run deep as well; your child may stand up for others or insist that rules be followed, even when it's inconvenient. These qualities can become strengths with the proper support and encouragement.

It's easy to get stuck seeing "challenging" behaviors as problems to stamp out. But if you look closer, these behaviors often have a purpose or meaning. A child who flaps their hands when excited isn't being stubborn; they're regulating their emotions. A kid who resists noisy birthday parties isn't antisocial; they're avoiding sensory overload that feels painful or scary. Even repetitive scripting of movie lines can be a way to practice language or self-soothe under stress. When you recognize the reasons behind these actions, you can respond with empathy rather than frustration. You shift from asking "How do I stop this?" to "What is my child telling me?" This small change opens up new possibilities for connection and problem-solving.

Instead of focusing on fixing differences, try supporting and celebrating them. If your child's favorite subject is weather patterns, use that interest to teach math or reading. Build routines around special interests, maybe weather flashcards for spelling practice or bar graphs with rainfall data. Shared interests are also powerful bridges for connection; joining your child in their passion, even briefly each day, sends a message: "I see you and I value what lights you up." When learning feels fun and meaningful, growth follows naturally.

Language matters as much as action. You'll hear debates about whether to say, "autistic child" (identity-first language) or "child with autism" (person-first language). There's no single answer that fits every family, but many autistic advocates prefer identity-first. They view autism as part of who they are, much like being tall or left-handed, rather than something added on later. Person-first language may feel safer to some families at first, especially if you're new to this world, but it can sometimes suggest separation or shame about the diagnosis. The most respectful choice is to use the language your child prefers as they grow up and to stay open to learning from autistic voices about what feels right for them. The key is always respect and individuality, seeing your child as more than any label.

If you start seeing neurodiversity in action each day, you'll find new ways to nurture your child's strengths while giving real support for their most challenging moments. You'll notice that what makes your child different is often what makes them shine brightly, even when that brightness sometimes comes with challenges. From the way they organize toys to how they ask questions about the world, their brain brings something valuable, something worth celebrating, not erasing.

Debunking Myths—Separating Fact from Fiction About Autism

If you're raising an autistic child, you've probably heard all kinds of myths from neighbors, relatives, or even well-meaning professionals. The flood of misinformation can be overwhelming and discouraging. One myth that stubbornly resurfaces is the idea that vaccines cause autism. This claim has been repeatedly debunked by numerous large-scale scientific studies worldwide. Yet, some parents still hear it whispered at playgroups or see it shared in online forums. Not only does this myth cause needless guilt and anxiety for parents, but it also distracts from understanding what autism truly is, a natural difference in brain development, not something caused by an injection or any single event. Relying on science and credible sources is vital. You can confidently say, "Decades of research show no link between vaccines and autism," and know you are standing on solid ground.

Another damaging stereotype is that autistic children lack empathy. I've seen this myth hurt families deeply, especially when teachers or relatives comment that a child "doesn't care how others feel." In reality, many autistic people experience emotions very intensely, sometimes so much that they become overwhelmed and shut down or withdraw. They may express empathy differently, perhaps through quiet gestures, shared interests, or simply being nearby when someone is upset. One mother I worked with described how her son would silently place his favorite toy beside his crying sister, unable to offer words but determined to comfort her. His empathy was genuine, albeit expressed in his own unique way. When you hear someone say, "Autistic kids don't feel for others," you might respond, "Empathy looks different for everyone, and my child shows care in ways that are just as meaningful."

You'll also come across the belief that all autistic people are the same. This myth couldn't be further from the truth. Autism is a spectrum, which means no two children are identical in the way they think, learn, or communicate. One child might speak early but struggle with changes in routine; another could be non-verbal yet master puzzles with ease. Some children love hugs, while others shrink from touch. Even among siblings with the same diagnosis, personalities and needs can be radically different. One parent I know has twins, one loves singing in front of crowds, while the other prefers quiet corners and headphones. When someone claims, "You've met one autistic person, you've met them all," remind them, "Autism is as varied as any group of people; each person brings their own strengths and struggles."

Other myths float around too, like the idea that autism is caused by bad parenting (it's not), or that children will "grow out of it" (autism is lifelong, though support needs may change). Some believe that autistic people can't form friendships or lead fulfilling lives. These ideas are not only wrong, but also harmful. They undermine your child's confidence and discourage families from seeking support or celebrating progress.

Misinformation can come from any direction: a family friend who means well but repeats outdated tales, a grandparent who worries about blame, or even a medical professional stuck in outdated thinking. When faced with these moments, having a prepared response can help you stay calm and protect your child's dignity. For example:

- "Actually, current research shows autism is not caused by vaccines or parenting style."
- "My child expresses feelings differently, but that doesn't mean he doesn't care."

- "Every autistic person is unique; what helps one child may not work for another."

These scripts can help ease tension and foster better understanding, rather than leading to arguments.

Outdated beliefs do real harm. They can delay diagnosis, block access to services, and make parents feel isolated or ashamed. Families sometimes avoid seeking help because they fear judgment or blame. Children may sense the stigma and begin to doubt their own worth. On the other hand, accurate knowledge is empowering. The more you understand about what autism really is, and isn't, the more you can advocate for your child and help others do the same.

When families share their real stories, myths start to fall apart. I've seen parents describe moments of connection, a non-speaking child gently stroking a parent's arm when they're sad; a young girl who memorizes every birthday in her class so she never misses a celebration; a teenager who stands up for classmates facing bullying. These moments matter because they reveal what's possible when we look beyond stereotypes.

Knowledge is power here. The more we speak up against falsehoods, the more space we create for our children to thrive as their authentic selves. Armed with facts and a little courage, you can help shift the conversation wherever you go.

Building "My Child's Profile"—Tracking Strengths, Triggers, and Preferences

Understanding your child goes far beyond a diagnosis or a checklist. One of the most powerful things you can do is build a living, breathing profile that paints an accurate picture of who your child is, what lights them up, what calms them, when they struggle, and how they shine. Think of this as your child's personal "owner's manual," a resource you can lean on and share with those who support your family. It's not about filling out forms for the sake of paperwork; it's about naming what matters most to your child in everyday life.

Start with the basics: what helps your child feel safe, what makes them smile, and what turns a smooth day upside down. Write down their favorite activities. Some children love water play or swinging at the park; others could spend hours flipping through picture books or lining up action figures. List comfort objects that bring peace, such as a worn blanket, a chewy necklace, or headphones for loud places. Jot down motivators that get your child engaged. Maybe it's bubbles, a five-minute turn on the tablet, or dancing to a favorite song. Don't forget to include sensory preferences: does your child seek out deep pressure hugs or avoid sticky textures? Do they light up at the sound of music but cover their ears in crowded spaces? These details matter.

To help you get started, here's a simple template you can use or adapt for your own family:

Sample "All About Me" Worksheet

- My name:
- My favorite things:
- Things that make me feel happy:
- Things that make me feel worried or upset:
- My comfort items:
- How I like to communicate (words, pictures, gestures, devices):
- What helps when I am upset:
- Foods I love (and foods I avoid):
- My superpowers (what I am great at):

This profile shouldn't just highlight challenges or needs. Make a point to include strengths, quirky senses of humor, intense focus on trains or animals, and kindness with pets or siblings. These "bright spots" can sometimes go unnoticed in the rush to manage daily struggles, but they are vital for self-esteem and for guiding teachers and therapists in connecting with your child.

Alongside strengths, track what triggers stress, meltdowns, or shutdowns. Stressors are often tied to sensory overload (like bright lights in a supermarket), changes in routine, or unclear expectations. Try using a daily log for a week or two to see if it helps. Note what happened just before your child became upset. Was it a loud noise? A transition from one activity to another? Being asked to do something unexpected? Rate the level of distress on a scale from 1 to 5. Patterns often emerge when you review these notes over several days.

Here's an example of what a daily log entry might look like:

- 8:00 AM: Refused breakfast, threw spoon—kitchen crowded and noisy (distress level 3).
- 11:30 AM: Calm during story time with weighted blanket (distress level 1).
- 2:00 PM: Meltdown after playground—unexpected fire alarm (distress level 5), covered ears, and hid under the table.
- 6:00 PM: Happy building towers with dad (distress level 1).

Use short notes and keep them simple; consistency matters more than detail overload. Over time, you'll see what helps to soothe your child and where extra support is needed. Invite your child to help identify their own triggers and comforts, if possible. Even very young children can point to pictures or use gestures to show what they like or dislike.

Don't lose sight of progress. It's easy to get caught up in tracking setbacks and forget the moments when things go right: a first wave hello at school drop-off, eating new food without protest, or trying a new game with a sibling. Create "success snapshots" by jotting down these wins in a notebook or on your phone. Include photos if possible; sometimes looking back on these bright spots helps build hope on tough days.

Sharing this profile is a game-changer for collaboration. Bring copies to school meetings or therapy sessions. Give one to babysitters or grandparents before a visit. When everyone is on the same page about what helps and what hinders, your child gets consistency and understanding everywhere they go. Teachers appreciate knowing that headphones can help during assemblies, while therapists can tailor sessions around favorite interests, such as dinosaurs or trains. Even family members who struggle to connect will find it easier when they have practical tips in hand.

Over the years, I've seen profiles like these open doors, turning frustration into compassion, confusion into clarity. They remind everyone involved that your child is more than a list of challenges; they're an individual with unique rhythms, joys, and ways of seeing the world.

Navigating the Diagnosis Journey—Scripts, Questions, and Action Steps

The moment you realize you need answers, things can start to feel overwhelming. The pathway from first concerns to a formal diagnosis is rarely straightforward. It can be filled with paperwork, waiting lists, and conversations that are both hopeful and intimidating. Knowing what to expect can help alleviate some of the uncertainty and anxiety associated with the unknown. Typically, the process begins with sharing your observations and concerns with your child's primary doctor. From there, you might be referred to developmental specialists, speech-language therapists, or psychologists. Some families begin by going through the educational system, pursuing evaluations through their local school district. Others follow a medical route, working with pediatricians who can refer them to specialty clinics. Each step, making that first call, filling out screening questionnaires, attending assessments, brings its own set of questions and emotions.

A timeline typically looks like this: initial concern, documentation and tracking at home, first conversation with a professional, screening appointments (such as the M-CHAT-R for toddlers), referrals to specialists, a full diagnostic assessment, and finally, feedback about the diagnosis and next steps. It's not unusual for this process to stretch over several months. Some parents encounter long waiting lists or need to push for second opinions if their concerns are minimized. An easy-to-follow flowchart can help visualize this sequence—imagine a simple series of boxes: Noticing Concerns → Talk to Doctor/Teacher → Screening Tool Used → Referral to Specialist → Formal Assessment → Diagnosis and Recommendations. Keeping this sequence in mind helps you set realistic expectations and prepares you for each phase of the process.

Reaching out for an evaluation can be daunting if you're unsure of what to say. Scripts can help you break the ice and focus on facts instead of feelings alone. For instance, when contacting your child's doctor or a specialist's office, try something like: "Hello, I'm calling because I have some concerns about my child's development. I've noticed specific things, such as limited eye contact and little use of words, at the age of two. I'd like to request an autism evaluation or referral to a developmental specialist." If you're following up by email, keep it brief but specific: "Dear Dr. Smith, I am concerned about my son's social communication. He rarely responds to his name or points to objects at 18 months. Could we discuss an autism assessment at our next appointment?" These clear examples effectively underscore your observations, avoiding the pitfalls of medical jargon and emotional overwhelm.

When meeting with professionals, have a set of focused questions ready. Ask what assessments will be used and what kinds of specialists will be involved. "Can you explain what the assessment process will involve?" or "Who will be present during the evaluation?" are good starters. After the assessment, don't hesitate to ask for details about the results: "What does this diagnosis mean for my child's daily life? What supports are available in our area? Are there specific therapies you recommend?" If you feel uncertain or something isn't clear, it's absolutely okay to ask for more explanation or for information in writing.

Receiving a diagnosis brings a storm of emotions, relief that you finally have answers, grief for expectations that may need adjusting, confusion about what comes next, and sometimes guilt about missing earlier signs. Each feeling is valid. Parents often worry they might have overlooked something or done something wrong; others feel overwhelmed by the amount of information suddenly presented to them. It's essential to acknowledge that there's no perfect reaction; processing these feelings requires time and support.

Once you have a diagnosis (or even if you're still waiting but know that additional help is needed), concrete next steps can provide a sense of direction. One of the first steps is to connect with your local early intervention service. These teams specialize in supporting young children and can help coordinate speech therapy, occupational therapy, or behavioral supports based on your child's profile. Most states and regions have designated agencies that serve children under three; for older kids, the local school district usually takes over coordination.

Building your support system is equally vital. Look for online communities where parents share tips and encouragement. Facebook groups, local meetups, or national organizations often offer forums or helplines. These spaces can be lifelines on tough days when you need advice or just want to know someone else who understands your world.

Create a folder or digital file to store all reports, assessment summaries, and official letters related to your child. Organization makes future appointments smoother and ensures no detail gets lost in the shuffle. This paperwork will come in handy at future school meetings or therapy visits, helping everyone stay on the same page.

This phase is marked by uncertainty and waiting, but it also signals a new chapter, a time when your child's unique needs are finally recognized and understood. No matter how bumpy the path feels right now, every step equips you with more knowledge and tools for your family's future together.

Chapter 2: Creating Connection—Strengthening Bonds Through Responsive Communication

Tuning In—Reading Your Child's Signals and Nonverbal Cues

Some mornings, you can sense the mood in the air before a single word is spoken. Maybe your child bounces into the kitchen, eyes wide and shoulders loose, or perhaps they slip quietly under the table, their faces turned away. Long before language emerges, children, especially autistic children, share their inner world through a rich tapestry of signals. These cues can be fleeting or bold, obvious or mysterious. Learning to notice and interpret them is one of the most important ways to connect with your child.

Every child has a unique "language" composed of expressions, movements, sounds, and energy shifts. Maybe your son wrinkles his nose and looks sideways when overwhelmed. Perhaps your daughter rubs her hands together when she wants attention, or hums softly to self-soothe. Some children flap their hands in delight, while others clench their jaws when anxious. Even the smallest detail, flicker in the eyes, a sudden stillness, a sharp intake of breath, are packed with meaning. If you pay attention to these moments, you begin to see a pattern: facial expressions morphing in sync with mood changes, feet tapping faster when excitement rises, or shoulders tightening just before tears appear.

Attunement is about meeting your child right where they are, not where you wish they were. It's easy to fall into the trap of expecting eye contact or certain gestures because "that's what kids do." But autistic children often show connection in different ways. Your child may not always look at you directly or answer when spoken to, but they might glance your way when you laugh, shift closer when you're calm, or mimic your actions out of the corner of their eye. Instead of focusing on what's "missing," tune in to the alternate channels your child uses. Attunement means noticing these signals and responding without judgment or pressure, which builds trust and lets your child know they are accepted as they are.

One powerful way to show understanding is through mirroring. When your child claps their hands or rocks gently, try echoing that motion, subtly, not mockingly. If they let out a joyful squeal at the sight of bubbles, join in with your own sound or movement. Mirroring says, "I see you. I get it." This can be especially comforting for a child who struggles with spoken words. At other times, respect for space is the most loving response. If your child pulls away or covers their ears, honor that boundary. Step back physically but stay emotionally available, letting them know you're close by if needed. This balance of mirroring and respecting space builds safety over time.

Picking up on subtle cues takes practice. Start by observing your child in various settings, such as playtime at home, crowded stores, and quiet moments before bed. Notice how their energy shifts throughout the day. Does a certain toy bring out smiles or focused concentration? Do group settings lead to fidgeting or withdrawal? Document these patterns in a simple daily communication journal or log. Write short notes: "Smiled and bounced in chair after music," "Turned away when brother shouted," "Tugged ear before meltdown." These notes help you identify recurring themes, what sparks joy, and what signals stress, providing valuable insights for teachers or therapists.

For some families, photos or video clips provide an additional layer of understanding. A quick phone video of your child lining up blocks or glancing at you during play can reveal subtle expressions or gestures that you might miss in real time. Reviewing these clips together as a family can spark new insights ("Did you see how she reached out when the music started?"). These visual records not only track progress but also help others, such as grandparents, teachers, and therapists, understand your child's communication style.

Try This: Communication Pattern Tracker

Set aside five minutes each evening to jot down two or three signals your child used that day to communicate. Include facial expressions (smiles, frowns), body language (turning away, leaning in), and vocalizations (humming, giggling). Note what happened just before and after each signal. Over a week or two, look for patterns: Does your child stiffen before loud noises? Do they move closer during quiet activities? This tracker can reveal hidden strengths and stressors, helping you respond more effectively.

Recognizing these patterns helps you respond with intention rather than guesswork. When you acknowledge your child's cues, smiling back at a glance, pausing when hands cover ears, you show respect for their way of connecting. Over time, this builds a foundation of trust that goes deeper than words alone ever could.

The Power of Play—Connection Before Correction

Children with autism often engage in activities like spinning a train wheel, lining up blocks by color, or repeating simple routines. Well-meaning adults may try to redirect or suggest "better" ways to play, but for autistic children, play is a crucial form of communication. Rather than correcting or directing, start by observing what truly interests your child: dinosaurs, keys, the sound of marbles, or anything else that draws their focus. These interests are opportunities for connection, not obstacles. When you join your child in their chosen activity, you affirm, "What interests you matters to me," meeting them in a place where they feel safe and seen.

Child-led play is distinct from adult-directed play. Instead of organizing and leading an activity, enter your child's play world as a supportive guest. If your child lines up cars, sit beside them and line up your own. Match their tempo and subtly copy their patterns. Spin the lids, sort the buttons, or stack blocks just as they do. Talking is optional; often, your presence and participation are enough to invite shared attention. Over time, you might notice your child glancing to see if you're copying correctly or offering you a turn - small but meaningful gestures of connection that go beyond planned "teachable moments."

Special interests serve as bridges for meaningful interaction. If your child loves sharks or knows every construction vehicle by heart, use these passions to connect. Build together with blocks, narrate stories about their favorite topics, or simply participate in play routines, however repetitive or unusual. Respecting and joining these interests validates your child's perspective. Even if play looks different from what you see with other children, that's fine. Parallel play, where you sit side by side, each focused on your own activity, still fosters connection. For many autistic kids, it feels less overwhelming than direct interaction and can lead to deeper engagement later.

Sensory play offers another path to connection, especially for children who avoid typical games or struggle with conversation. Simple activities, such as pouring water, squishing playdough, running hands through sand, and playing with bubbles, invite participation without requiring words. Take turns filling buckets, use cookie cutters together, or simply share the experience of repetitive actions. Join your child in their routines rather than trying to change them. Sometimes a simple narration ("You're scooping! I'm scooping too!") is enough to foster togetherness.

Parents often worry about repetition, strict routines, or the lack of pretend play. Instead of seeing these patterns as issues, consider them ways for your child to find comfort or process the world at their own pace. If your child repeats an activity, ask yourself what they gain from it and gently build on what they are already doing. For example, if they always build towers a certain way, try stacking next to theirs with different colors or add a playful sound effect if your tower falls. These variations can encourage curiosity without disrupting their sense of security.

Avoid peppering play with questions or directing every step ("What color is this? What does the cow say?"). Too many questions can be overwhelming. Stick to narrating your actions: "I'm making a tall tower! Oh no, it fell." This commentary invites your child into a shared experience, without putting pressure on them to respond. When they're ready for something new, offer gentle invitations: "Can my car drive next to yours?" or "Want to pour water into this bowl?" If they decline or ignore you, respect their choice and keep participating on their terms.

Some days, your child may refuse all invitations and seem absorbed in their own world. That's normal, just being quietly present is enough. Other times, a glance, a smile, or a brief moment of shared action shows that connection is happening in their own way and timing.

Play isn't just practice for future learning; it is real learning. Every shared game, parallel block-stack, sensory ritual, or repeated action helps your child feel valued and understood. This foundation of trust will support all future communication, as your child grows more confident with words and social play.

Responsive Communication—Mirroring, Modeling, and Wait Time

Responsive communication is more than just talking at your child and hoping something clicks; it's about creating a back-and-forth rhythm, even if words aren't part of the exchange yet. When your child makes a sound, gesture, or tries out a new word, how you respond can open a door to new learning or quietly shut it. For autistic children, feeling heard and understood starts with these moments. Every attempt, whether it's a shout, a clap, a single syllable, or a curious look, counts as communication. When you meet your child's effort with attention and encouragement rather than correction or pressure, you plant the seeds for language to grow.

Mirroring is one of the most powerful tools you have, and it's surprisingly simple to use. If your child claps their hands, you clap too. If they say "buh" while looking at a ball, repeat "buh" and show interest in the ball. Some children screech, bang toys, or tap out rhythms; joining them (at a similar volume and pace) shows that you notice what matters to them. This isn't about being silly or mocking, it's about saying "I see you" in a form that makes sense to your child. A toddler who sees you echo their movements or sounds is more likely to feel safe enough to try again and again. Even older children who use only a handful of words can benefit from this approach. Mirroring validates their efforts and builds confidence.

Modeling language is the next key step. Instead of demanding your child repeat words after you or correcting their speech every time, focus on showing them what communication can look like in context. Suppose your child points to the fridge and says "juice." Rather than launching into a quiz ("What do you want? Say 'I want juice'!"), you simply expand on their effort: "Oh, juice! You want some juice?" or "Yes, cold orange juice." If they say "truck," you might add, "Big blue truck!" or "The truck goes vroom." This technique gives your child real-life examples of how words fit together without the stress of getting it "right." It's about exposure, not perfection. Over time, hearing these natural expansions helps kids absorb new vocabulary and sentence structure.

Some days, your child may only make sounds or offer part of a word. Meet them where they are; respond enthusiastically but avoid turning every moment into a lesson. If your child says "ba!" while rolling a ball, you can say, "Ball! Rolling the ball!" But if they don't respond right away or echo back, that's okay. The key is to keep language flowing without expectation. Modeling works just as well with gestures or signs as with spoken words, if your child points to a picture in a book, you point too and name it together. For children using AAC devices or picture cards, demonstrate how to use them naturally during daily routines. Instead of prompting "Press 'eat'!" at snack time, model pressing "eat" yourself while saying, "I'm going to eat crackers."

One of the trickiest skills for adults is giving wait time, pausing after you say something to allow your child space to process and respond.

Many kids with autism need more time to organize their thoughts or coordinate the motor skills needed for words or gestures. After asking a question or modeling language, silently count to five in your head before repeating or moving on. This pause might feel awkward at first, especially if you're used to quick back-and-forth chatter. But those extra seconds can make all the difference. Sometimes your child will surprise you with a delayed response, a word, a point, or even eye contact, when given enough time.

Visual supports can make wait time less stressful for both you and your child. Use simple pictures, objects, or gestures alongside your words to make your message clear and easy to follow. For instance, hold up a snack choice while asking, "Apple or banana?" and give plenty of time for your child to point or reach. If you're waiting for them to choose an activity, show two toys and pause expectantly rather than repeating the question over and over. This quiet encouragement tells your child that their input matters and that communication doesn't have to be rushed.

Some days, no amount of mirroring or modeling will spark an obvious response, and that's okay too. The goal isn't constant conversation but consistent presence and support. Celebrate every attempt at communication, no matter how small. A glance, a tap on the table, a whispered sound, all deserve acknowledgment. Over time, this approach helps children feel safe trying new ways of expressing themselves.

You don't need fancy words or formal training; just watch, listen, echo back, offer gentle expansions, and wait patiently for whatever comes next. These moments build the sturdy foundation for language and trust that will grow alongside your child's confidence.

Scripting and Echolalia—Harnessing Repetition for Understanding

If you've noticed your child quoting cartoon lines repeatedly or echoing words back to you instead of answering, you're seeing scripting and echolalia in action. These behaviors may puzzle or frustrate parents, but they serve real communication purposes for autistic children. Scripting occurs when a child uses lines from media or past conversations, whereas echolalia involves repeating words or phrases, either immediately after hearing them (immediate echolalia) or sometime later (delayed echolalia). Both are common ways autistic children process language, express feelings, and connect, even if it doesn't resemble typical conversation.

It's a misconception that scripting and echolalia are just mindless parroting. In reality, repetition helps many autistic children practice language, process new experiences, or handle strong emotions. For instance, a child who shouts, "To infinity and beyond!" is using a familiar phrase to express excitement or share in a moment, not just echoing Buzz Lightyear. Scripts can help children self-soothe or bring routine to unpredictable situations, and sometimes they act as placeholders when a child wants to participate but can't find their own words yet. Recognizing the reasons behind repetition can change your response; instead of seeing these behaviors as "wrong," you can approach them as opportunities for connection.

Recognizing Patterns and Building Bridges

Pay attention to when and how your child uses certain scripts. Do they say "I need backup!" when frustrated or "All aboard!" to signal they want to leave? These phrases reveal your child's needs, interests, and emotions. Personalized scripts for everyday routines can be especially helpful. For tricky transitions, create simple phrases together, like "All done!" to finish an activity or "I need help" for challenges. Practice these during calm moments, connecting scripts to real situations. Over time, your child may use these phrases more flexibly and with more people.

Expanding Scripted Language

Turning scripts into functional language takes patience. Movie lines or echoed phrases aren't static; they can evolve into useful social scripts. For example, if your child loves saying "Let's get this show on the road!"

before leaving, you might pair it with a practical phrase: "That means it's time to go. Can you try saying 'Let's go!' as we put on our coats?" If your child echoes a question you've asked ("Do you want juice?"), model the answer: "Juice! Yes, please." Over time, your child may start to use the new response independently.

Supporting Flexibility and Growth

Don't expect overnight changes. Some children may hold on to their favorite scripts, while others will try new words when they feel comfortable. Encourage flexibility by offering choices or alternatives; after your child says, "To the Batmobile!" you could suggest, "Or maybe 'Time to go!'" Add gestures or visual aids to clarify the meaning, and celebrate any attempt to use language differently, no matter how small.

Responding Supportively

Avoid shaming or shutting down repetitive language. Criticizing or insisting on "real words" can backfire, making children anxious to try. Instead, acknowledge the script ("I hear you say 'No more monkeys jumping on the bed!' when you're feeling silly") and gently model other options ("We can say 'Let's be silly!' too"). If scripting is a comfort after a tough day, join in for a bit before offering something new. This respects your child's process and guides them toward broader interactions.

Navigating Scripting in Social Settings

If scripting disrupts learning or socializing, like loud repetition during class, redirect calmly. Offer a quiet time or place for scripting or set specific times for movie lines. Visual cues can help remind your child, and working with teachers ensures your child isn't punished but supported in managing scripting.

Scripting and echolalia aren't just quirks; they're vital communication tools. By treating these behaviors as meaningful, you help your child build language skills and confidence at their own pace. When you view repetition as a resource, not a roadblock, you foster connection and growth in new ways.

Building Trust During Meltdowns—Co-Regulation Techniques

When your child's emotions spill over and the meltdown starts, it's like watching a storm arrive. You can sense the tension, feel the shift in the room, and sometimes all you can do is stay steady. For autistic children, meltdowns aren't tantrums or a bid for attention. They're a response to overwhelming stress, sensory overload, or frustration that words can't reach. Your nervous system is wired to connect with your child's, and science refers to this as co-regulation. If you stay as calm as possible in the chaos, your own steady breathing and gentle presence can signal safety to your child's nervous system. You are providing the anchor when they feel like they're drifting in rough waters.

During a meltdown, don't rush to talk things through or solve the problem. Words can feel like noise when a child's brain is flooded with stress. Instead, focus on quiet actions and presence. Sit beside your child, not in front of them, respecting their space while showing you're close if needed. You might sit silently on the floor, hands open in your lap, body turned slightly away to reduce pressure. Sometimes, simply being there without words is enough to offer comfort. If your child reaches for you or seeks physical closeness, offer a favorite stuffed animal or blanket, or gently place it nearby. Familiar objects can be powerful signals of safety and predictability in the middle of upheaval.

Some children need nonverbal support even more than spoken comfort. Try matching your breathing to a slow, even rhythm. If your child glances at you or starts to notice your breaths, exaggerate the motion by just slightly slowing the inhale and a longer exhale. This can help regulate both of you. For children who tolerate touch, a gentle hand on the back or shoulder (only if welcomed) can be a grounding experience. If touch isn't right, simply staying close by is still meaningful. Keep your movements minimal and predictable; sudden gestures or loud noises can add to the overwhelm.

You might also experiment with co-regulation techniques that don't involve talking at all. Humming softly, rocking gently side-to-side (if your child finds it calming), or offering a cool washcloth can sometimes break through the intensity without requiring direct interaction. If your child wants space, pushing you away or hiding under a table, respect that need while staying within eyesight if possible. You can say softly, "I'm here if you need me," then allow them room to recover without pressing for engagement.

Scripts are helpful for uncertain moments: "I see you're upset. I'll sit right here." Or simply, "You're safe. I'm not going anywhere." After the storm passes and your child begins to quiet down, maybe their breathing slows, their muscles relax, or they look around. Don't rush into explanations or lectures. Instead, offer reassurance: "That was really tough. I'm here." This simple validation tells your child their feelings matter and that you are a safe presence no matter what.

Repairing after a meltdown is just as important as surviving it. When everyone is calm again, circle back with gentle acknowledgment. You could say, "That felt really big. It's okay to feel mad or scared. We got through it together." If your child is open to it, consider snuggling or sharing a quiet activity, such as drawing together, reading a favorite book, or simply lying side by side and listening to music. These moments rebuild trust and help your child understand that meltdowns don't break your bond; instead, they are opportunities to prove that your love is steady and unconditional.

For yourself as much as for your child, remember that meltdowns are not failures; they are part of living with intense feelings and sensory experiences. Your job isn't to prevent every meltdown but to provide safety during and after. Over time, your calm presence teaches your child that big feelings aren't dangerous; they're manageable because someone wise and steady is right there alongside them.

Using Social Stories—Preparing for Change and New Experiences

Change can be challenging for autistic children, as new experiences often bring uncertainty. Even positive events, such as a fun outing or starting a new class, can cause anxiety simply because they are unfamiliar. Social stories are practical tools that prepare your child for these unknowns by explaining what will happen, what to expect, and how to respond. They break down new routines and social demands into small, manageable steps, often using words, photos, or drawings to make abstract ideas more concrete, helping your child face change with greater confidence.

You don't need to be a professional writer to create helpful social stories at home. Use a simple template: set the scene, outline the sequence of events, mention possible feelings, and finish with reassurance. A dental visit story might go: "On Thursday, we will drive to Dr. Patel's office. We will wait and read a book. The dentist will count my teeth. If I feel nervous, Mom will hold my hand. When we're done, we'll go home together." Including real photos of the office exterior, waiting room, or dentist helps make the experience feel tangible and predictable.

Social stories are especially valuable for major transitions, such as the first day of school or starting a new activity. For instance: "On Monday, I will start at Pine Street School. My teacher is Ms. Lee. I'll bring my backpack and see other children. Sometimes it may feel loud or busy. If I need a break, I can tell Ms. Lee or go to the quiet corner." Add photos of the building, classroom, and teacher when possible. Read the story together, leading up to the event. Repetition builds familiarity and eases anxiety.

Visual support is an important complement to these stories. Use printed photos from your phone or search online for relevant images; even stick figures or simple drawings work if photos aren't available. The key is context. Reading the same story several times is not a problem; repetition provides comfort and a sense of predictability. Use positive language, focusing on what your child *can* do, rather than what they cannot. For example, rather than "I won't cry," say, "If I feel worried, I can hold my fidget toy or squeeze Mom's hand."

If your child loses interest or becomes disengaged, adjust the story. Shorten sentences, use more pictures, or convert the story into a comic strip for older kids. Some children enjoy personalizing their stories by drawing or selecting images, which increases their sense of ownership and investment.

Not all social stories are effective immediately. If your child seems confused, check whether the language and images are age-appropriate or relevant to their interests; adjust accordingly. Sometimes, including sensory details (how things sound, smell, or feel) or involving family members in acting out the story can help reinforce its message.

Introduce new social stories when your child is calm and undistracted, not right before leaving or during a stressful moment. Read together in a quiet place with a steady, gentle tone. Pause at key images or ask simple questions, like "What do you think you'll see first?" Allow your child to respond in their own way, even if it's just a look or a word.

For children who thrive on routine, social stories can help with both everyday transitions and significant changes. You can write stories about any event, such as getting a haircut, visiting relatives, celebrating birthdays, or trying new foods. Over time, these stories become familiar scripts your child can rely on when feeling overwhelmed.

As you finish this chapter on connection and communication, remember that each small step, whether it's shared play, a quiet moment, or preparing with a social story, helps build trust and understanding between you and your child. These efforts strengthen bonds and support your child's growth. Next, we'll explore practical strategies to make daily routines smoother for both of you as you navigate each day together.

Chapter 3: Communication for All—Tools, Tech, and Strategies to Support Every Child

Choosing the Right Communication Tools—AAC, PECS, and More

If you've noticed your child struggling to express wants or feelings, you're not alone. Watching a child try to connect without the right tools can feel overwhelming, but it's important to remember that communication is much broader than just speech. There are many ways for children to express themselves; the key is finding what works best for your child.

Communication supports range widely, and no single system fits everyone. There are AAC (Augmentative and Alternative Communication) devices, PECS (Picture Exchange Communication System), low-tech communication boards, sign language, and speech-generating apps, among others. Some children use only one method, while others benefit from a combination of methods. The goal is for your child to find a "voice," whether through a tablet, exchanging pictures, using gestures, or speaking.

AAC devices come in various forms, including high-tech tablets with apps like Proloquo2Go, speech-generating machines, and even simple laminated picture cards. These help users communicate by turning selections into spoken words or phrases. PECS is a structured system where kids exchange pictures for desired items, gradually building more complex ways of expressing themselves. Communication boards or books offer a set of images or symbols that children can point to for specific needs, such as "toilet," "help," or their favorite snacks. Some respond well to sign language, especially if they're gesture-oriented; others may prefer speech buttons that play a recorded message when pressed.

Choosing the right tool depends on your child's strengths, challenges, and interests. Are they drawn to pictures or technology? Can they point to or touch icons? Do they enjoy exchanging objects? These preferences help narrow down choices. It's wise to try different supports and see which ones spark your child's engagement. Some kids might dislike cards but love using an app, or vice versa.

Partnering with a speech-language pathologist (SLP) is essential. An SLP can assess your child's skills, try various options, and guide you towards what works best, based on factors like fine motor abilities, attention span, sensory sensitivities, and daily family routines. The objective isn't just to choose a tool, but to create a comprehensive system that seamlessly integrates into daily life, at home, in school, and in the community.

A frequent concern is that using AAC or PECS might prevent kids from learning to talk. Research shows the opposite is true, having alternative communication options reduces frustration and often encourages more speech and language development. When children succeed in expressing themselves, no matter the method, they're more motivated to interact. Some develop speech later as confidence grows; for others, AAC remains the main form of communication, and that's perfectly fine.

To help decide, consider your child's current abilities:

- If they use some words or gestures but struggle with phrases, try supplementing with communication boards or simple sign language.
- If they aren't speaking but are visually motivated, PECS or a picture book may be a good fit.
- Tech-savvy kids may find AAC apps more engaging. Take sensory preferences into account as well: some individuals dislike

laminated cards but enjoy pressing buttons, while others avoid screens but prefer tangible objects.

Interactive Element: Decision Flowchart for Communication Supports

- Is my child using any words?
    - Yes: Expand with communication boards/books and model short phrases.
    - No: Does my child point or gesture?
        - Yes: Try PECS or sign language.
        - No: Is the child drawn to technology?
            - Yes: Try AAC apps with touchscreens.
            - No: Explore object exchange systems or tactile boards.
- Does my child respond to pictures?
    - Yes: Use PECS or photo boards.
    - No: Try audio buttons or sign language.
- Are motor skills adequate for pointing/tapping?
    - Yes: Touchscreen apps.
    - No: Use large cards or partner-assisted scanning.

Mix and match tools as needed, PECS at home, AAC in school, signs with family. Adapt as your child grows. The best system is one your child uses to connect, even if it's not what you expected.

If you're feeling lost, remember this isn't about "fixing" your child, but giving them the chance to be heard. Communication is a right, and how it happens should fit your child's individuality. Every effort counts, and each breakthrough, small or big, is worth celebrating.

Introducing Visual Supports—Schedules, Choice Boards, and Timers

When you're raising or teaching a child who struggles with communication, the world can feel unpredictable. It's not just about words. It's about making life feel less chaotic and more manageable. Visual supports step in as a lifeline here, transforming uncertainty into something your child can see, touch, and predict. Whether your child talks or not, visuals bridge the gap between what's happening and what's expected; they can calm anxious moments, make transitions smoother, and help your child feel more independent.

If mornings at your house are usually a scramble, teeth-brushing battles, lost shoes, meltdowns over forgotten steps, a simple photo-based schedule can change the whole mood. Start by snapping pictures of each step: pajamas off, clothes on, breakfast at the table, and backpack by the door. Print the photos and line them up in order. Stick them to the fridge or a clipboard where your child can see and touch them. Point to each image as you go along; soon, your child may start pointing out what comes next. This approach works for any routine, bedtime, getting ready for school, even going to grandma's. For a portable twist, use a small album or keyring of pictures for outings.

First-then boards are another powerful tool. They work wonders for kids who resist change or struggle to finish non-preferred tasks. You show two visuals: "First wash hands (picture of a sink), then snack (picture of crackers)." This structure makes expectations concrete and manageable. Laminated cards attached with Velcro or magnets are sturdy enough for daily use and easy to swap out. Bring one along for errands: "First sit in the cart, then choose a treat." The more you use these boards, the more your child learns that good things follow hard things and that routines have an order they can trust.

Choice boards offer something just as valuable: control. Many autistic children feel powerless over their day. With a choice board, you lay out snack options ("apple," "banana," "crackers") or activities ("blocks," "puzzle," "outside"). Your child points, hands you the card, or simply gazes at their selection. This small act of choosing builds confidence and reduces power struggles because your child gets a say in what happens next.

You don't have to buy expensive materials. If you have a smartphone or tablet, explore visual schedule apps, many are customizable with your own photos or icons. An iPad can display a simple schedule that your child taps to move forward. Free apps allow you to design first-then boards or sequence activities using drag-and-drop icons. If tech isn't your thing, sticky notes on a whiteboard work beautifully for sequencing steps; peel them off as you go along. You can use magnets on the fridge with printed images or even draw simple stick figures on index cards if you're in a pinch.

Timers deserve a special spotlight here. Many children feel anxious about how long an activity will last or when it will end. A visual timer, anything from a basic kitchen timer to a colorful app that shows time "running out", can ease these worries. Set the timer for brushing teeth or waiting for a turn; show your child how the time shrinks away. Some kids prefer sand timers that they can flip over themselves. If they get stuck on watching the timer instead of doing the activity, try covering it partway or using an app that provides gentle sound cues instead of constant visual cues.

Sometimes visuals get ignored, ripped up, or become new obsessions. If your child ignores the supports, check if they're too complicated or overwhelming; simplify by using fewer steps or bigger images. If visuals become fixations (for example, your child wants to peel off all the cards instead of following them), set clear boundaries: "Cards stay on until we finish," and offer another fidget for their hands if needed. Rotate images frequently to keep them fresh and meaningful; invite your child to help select photos or colors, so they feel involved.

Introducing visuals takes patience and repetition. Don't be discouraged if your child doesn't respond right away or seems uninterested at first. Model using the schedule yourself: "Look, it's time for breakfast! Next up is shoes." Encourage siblings and caregivers to refer to the visuals too, consistently helps them stick. Celebrate small wins when your child checks off a step or makes a choice using the board.

As you experiment with different visual supports, keep notes about what sparks engagement and what falls flat. Each child's preferences shift over time; what works one month might need tweaking the next. Your creativity as a parent or teacher is more powerful than any fancy product on the market. Every photo you tape up, every card you laminate, is another way of saying: "I see you, I want to help you understand this world." That message is what really makes the difference.

Low-Tech Communication Hacks—Everyday Items for Big Impact

You don't need expensive gadgets to help your child communicate more clearly; everyday household items can often work best. The trick is to look around and see what can be repurposed for communication. For instance, a paper plate can become an instant feelings tool: draw a happy face on one side and a sad or frustrated face on the other. Now, your child can flip the plate to show how they're feeling, it's immediate, visual, and perfect when words are out of reach.

Clothespins can also be turned into "yes/no" or "more/all done" indicators. Write or color-code the answers on the clothespins and let your child clip them on a board or their shirt collar. These tactile tools give your child a concrete way to answer, which is especially valuable during stressful moments.

For something portable, try a keyring with laminated cards. Print or draw images for "drink," "toilet," "help," "break," "snack," etc., punch holes in the corners, and loop them on a keyring attached to a bag or backpack. This lets your child hand you the right card to communicate a need, preventing meltdowns and allowing more control over their day. One parent shared that a photo keychain allowed her son to signal when he wanted to leave grandma's, taking family visits from fraught to manageable.

Visual lanyards make communication tools even more accessible on the go. Attach small cards or mini-boards to a breakaway lanyard and wear it during outings. Some families personalize these with colors or stickers to make them appealing. For older kids, wallet-sized cards in lunchboxes or jackets also work well, especially on field trips or with substitute teachers. Even a single "I need help" card can be a lifeline during overwhelming times away from home.

The best part of these low-tech hacks is how quickly they can be created using supplies you already have. For a quick feelings chart, tape magazine cut-out faces to cardboard and hang it by the door. Use sticky notes in different colors on the fridge to track daily choices: blue for water, yellow for juice, and green for snacks. If your child is drawn to objects, keep a basket of small toys that represent activities: a car for outings, a spoon for meals, and a ball for playing. Handing you the item lets them express their needs without words.

To get started, decide on the key messages: "eat," "drink," "bathroom," "help," and "break" are good basics. Use clear, simple images and laminate them if possible (packing tape works, too). Punch holes to thread them onto a keyring, lanyard, or ribbon. Practice using them together in calm moments so it becomes natural, and include siblings and caregivers in practice so everyone is familiar with the system.

Keep supports wherever communication often breaks down, by the car seat, at the dinner table, at the bedside. For example, a zip-top bag of emotion faces in the car, or clothespins by the table to indicate when your child is finished eating. The aim isn't perfection but progress, giving your child options to express themselves without needing speech at all times.

Families often develop creative solutions tailored to their kids. One dad used a pillbox to sort outing photos, and each morning his daughter would open the right compartment to choose their activity. A mom put emotion stickers on her son's favorite stuffed animal so he could point to his current feeling. These clever hacks come from everyday creativity, not specialty stores.

The most important thing is that these communication aids be consistent and easily accessible; don't keep them tucked away for special times. Leave them out and remind teachers, relatives, and caregivers to use them. Send extras to school or grandparents' homes. Frequent use and availability make these tools truly effective.

Ultimately, every time you offer a low-tech option, you tell your child their voice matters, however it's expressed. Even the smallest successes, a card handed over, a plate flipped, lead to greater relief, understanding, and connection for both of you.

Making AAC Routine—Integrating Devices at Home and School

Integrating an AAC device into daily life requires intention, but it shouldn't feel like an extra burden. The device, or whichever tool your child uses, should be as present as a favorite toy or snack cup. If the AAC sits unused until therapy, it's just a gadget; if it's always nearby at the table, in the car, or during story time, it becomes a true voice. Families often treat the device like an extra limb: it goes in the grocery cart, sits on the bathroom counter, or joins at the dinner table. This predictability tells your child, "Your words matter all the time, not just during speech sessions."

Modeling AAC is powerful. Don't wait for your child to use the device, show them how by talking with it yourself. For example, during bath time, press "bath" or "water" on the device and describe what you're doing: "First, we take off socks. Now it's bath time!" During play, tap "blocks" or "build." At meals, use it to pick "milk" or "more." This method, called aided language input, mimics how children learn spoken words by hearing them used in context. When you use the device regularly, your child views it as a meaningful tool for sharing thoughts, rather than just a therapy prop, making it feel like a natural extension of their communication.

Embedding AAC into daily transitions and routines is key. Before going out, use the device to say "shoes," "outside," or "school." If your child struggles during transitions, model phrases like "wait," "help," or "finished." These moments don't need to be perfect; focus on making the device a regular part of your routines. Encourage everyone in the family to use the device. Siblings can press favorite words or choose activities. The more people participate, the more natural AAC becomes.

Consistency between home and school matters. Collaborate with teachers and therapists to ensure that everyone understands how the device works and its integration into classroom routines. A simple home-school log in your child's backpack, a notebook or digital document, lets teachers note which words or phrases were used, what went well, and any challenges. At home, you can add new vocabulary or note when your child uses the device independently. This back-and-forth helps everyone stay informed and builds momentum.

When sending an AAC device to school, do a quick daily check: Is it charged? Is the case secure? Are any new words needed for the day's activities? Pack a charger and extra stylus if you can. Remind school staff to keep the device within reach (not locked away), and encourage its use during group work, play, and transitions, not just structured lessons. Ask about storage in the classroom so devices don't get lost or left behind.

Bringing AAC into daily life isn't always smooth. Sometimes kids ignore the device; this is normal. Continue modeling without pressure and celebrate small steps: a glance at the screen, touching an icon, or simply carrying the device. If anyone feels awkward or thinks AAC is too slow, offer a quick demo. Show how using the device can speed up communication by reducing frustration. If the device is often dead, set a daily charging routine. Plug it in next to your phone each night.

If AAC use slips, perhaps due to boredom, glitches, or habit, refresh routines by adding new vocabulary linked to current interests (e.g., "T-

Rex," "stomp," or "roar" for a dinosaur phase). For tech issues, keep a backup board or a printed copy of the core words so communication can continue while waiting for repairs.

Above all, don't let perfectionism stall progress. It's okay if you sometimes forget to model or if your child only uses one button for a while. AAC is a living system that grows with practice, patience, and trial and error. Every effort you make, no matter how small, helps your child find their voice in meaningful ways.

Troubleshooting Communication Frustrations—Common Roadblocks and Fixes

It's common to feel frustrated when your child pushes aside their device, starts mashing buttons, or quickly loses interest in a new board or app. You might also encounter skepticism from others about the value of visuals or AAC. These bumps are normal; communication for autistic children, especially at first, rarely follows a smooth, steady path.

A frequent roadblock is outright refusal, your child ignores or rejects the device. This may signal a need for more control, frustration, or a sense of boredom. If the tool isn't fun or useful, most kids won't engage with it. Try making communication playful and low-pressure. Rather than demanding a response ("Say it on your talker!"), model enthusiasm: "Let's tell Dad 'cookie' on your talker!" Share silly requests or play favorite games. Sometimes, moving to a new location or using the device playfully (e.g., "Tell the dog to 'Sit!'") can reignite curiosity.

Button-mashing is another classic snag. For many children, this is exploration, not misbehavior. Use it as a learning opportunity: narrate what each button means ("You pressed 'cat'—cats say meow"). These build understanding, even if it's not yet perfect communication. If button-mashing becomes a routine behavior during specific times, such as before bed or when upset, it may be a sign of poor self-regulation. In those moments, lower demands and offer alternatives, such as a fidget or calming activity.

When your child loses interest after you've invested time and effort, don't force the tool. Revisit whether the system still fits your child's interests and needs. Refresh vocabulary with favorite foods, activities, or inside jokes. Let your child help choose new words or pictures. Keep the tools accessible but avoid pressing during stressful moments. Sometimes, seeing someone else use the tools naturally brings back interest.

Misunderstandings from others can be discouraging. Teachers might see AAC as too slow, or relatives may overlook your child's signals. Bring these adults in as partners: teach them to pause, use the tools themselves, and wait for your child's response. Scripts can help ("When Jamie taps 'help,' pause and check in"). Provide quick-reference visuals (like sticky notes) to remind caregivers of key cues.

During meltdowns or shutdowns, speech may be inaccessible. Visual scripts, like an "I need a break" card or a symbol on a device, can bridge the gap. Teach and model these tools during calm times ("I'm feeling stressed, I'll take a break"). Place them in visible, easily accessible locations at home, in the car, or at school. When your child is overwhelmed, gently offer a visual rather than pushing for words: "Would you like your break card?" This empowers your child to communicate effectively even during times of distress.

Remember, adults need troubleshooting support too. If progress stalls, gather your team, teachers, therapists, aides, and problem-solve together. Involve your child at their level: "Is there something you want to say that's missing?" or "Do you want different pictures?" Let your child help select symbols or words; even simple choices boost ownership and confidence.

Always celebrate any communication attempt, pressing one button, handing over a card, or pointing to a picture. Acknowledge effort with praise or a favorite reward, even if responses aren't perfect: "Thanks for telling me!" or an extra minute with a favorite toy reinforces that communication is valued.

Patience is essential. Progress may be slow, uneven, or invisible at first. Your child might reject a tool one week and love it the next. Stay flexible, try new ideas, and listen to feedback from your child and team. Frustration is normal for both you and your child; it's not a sign of failure. Communication is about building connections, not seeking perfection. Small steps make a bigger difference than you think.

Practical Exercise: Reflection Prompt

Think of three recent times your child struggled to communicate. What was the situation? What tools were available? Note what helped and what didn't. Then brainstorm a small change you could try next time: a new card, a quieter spot, or a favorite character on the board. Small, flexible adjustments often lead to meaningful progress.

Supporting Siblings as Communication Partners

Siblings can be the best teachers your child ever has, often in ways you don't expect. The bond between siblings is unique, full of inside jokes, quiet comfort, and sometimes loud squabbles. In families where one child is autistic and the other is not, this relationship takes on even more power. Brothers and sisters become natural models, showing language and social skills in ways that feel real, not forced. If you watch closely, you might notice your neurotypical child using a gesture or repeating a phrase to get their sibling's attention. These moments matter. Siblings who play and interact with each other make communication feel less like a lesson and more like part of daily life.

You can support this dynamic by inviting siblings to join in communication supports, whether it's an AAC device, visuals, or homemade tools. Try sibling-led "show and tell," where the older child uses the communication board to talk about a favorite toy, then encourages their autistic brother or sister to choose a symbol or press a button in return. These low-pressure games make learning enjoyable. Another easy activity is adapting turn-taking games, like rolling a ball or building with blocks, so that each player must use a card, switch, or device to signal "my turn" or "your turn." This teaches both kids the rhythm of back-and-forth conversation while giving your autistic child more chances to practice.

Siblings are often eager to help but may not always know what to do when their brother or sister communicates differently. As a parent, you can provide them with simple scripts that make things less confusing. For example, explain that "When your brother points to the train card, it means he wants to play trains with you." Or let them know that "If she uses her talker to say 'no,' you should respect it just like if she said it out loud." This sets clear expectations and helps siblings recognize nonverbal or alternative forms of communication as just as meaningful as speech.

It's essential to discuss openly stimming and other behaviors that may appear unusual. Children are naturally curious and may feel embarrassed if classmates stare at them in public. You can coach siblings with gentle responses: "When your sister flaps her hands, it means she's excited or calming down. You don't have to stop her, just let her be." These conversations foster empathy and inclusion within the family and beyond.

Sometimes, siblings feel a mix of pride, frustration, or even jealousy. It's normal for them to want your attention or wish things were easier. Maybe they're proud when their brother uses his device for the first time at dinner but upset when a meltdown interrupts their favorite show. Recognize these feelings without judgment. Set aside one-on-one time for each child when possible, even if it's just ten minutes reading together at bedtime. Family rituals can also be helpful: consider creating a weekly "communication champion" award for effort (not just success) or celebrate small victories with a group high-five or a special dessert. These rituals reinforce the idea that everyone's progress counts and help siblings feel recognized for their patience and support.

Encourage resilience by involving siblings in problem-solving when challenges arise. Ask for their ideas: "What could we do when your brother gets upset in the car?" or "How might we help your sister use her words when she's tired?" This inclusion makes them feel valued and gives them a sense of agency in family life.

Some days will be smooth, filled with laughter and teamwork; other days might end in tears and slammed doors. Both kinds of days are part of loving a sibling with differences. If you see rivalry brewing or one child pulling away, check in with them privately. A simple "It seems like today was hard, do you want to talk about it?" can open up honest dialogue.

Remember, siblings who learn early that communication comes in many forms often grow up more flexible, compassionate, and resourceful. They know firsthand that everyone has something valuable to say, even if it's said with pictures, buttons, or just a look.

As we conclude this chapter on building communication for every child, remember that siblings are not just helpers; they're partners in growth. The home you shape now becomes the foundation for empathy and inclusion far beyond your walls. Next, we'll explore nurturing independence, helping your child take confident steps toward developing daily skills and self-advocacy.

Chapter 4: Calming the Storm—Meltdown Management and Emotional Regulation

Understanding Meltdowns vs. Tantrums—What's Really Happening?

Imagine you're in line at a crowded store, half-packing groceries, when your child suddenly collapses to the floor, wailing. Shoppers stare, and you feel exposed. In that moment, you wonder: is this a tantrum or something deeper? This distinction is crucial, not just for managing the situation, but for truly helping your child.

On the surface, meltdowns and tantrums can look similar, but inside your child, very different things are happening. A tantrum is typically intentional, driven by a desire for a specific toy, candy, or the opportunity to stay up late. It's goal-oriented. Kids having tantrums might pause to see if you're watching or intensify the show if they get attention. Tantrums usually subside if the goal is achieved or if you remain calm and consistent, without giving in.

Meltdowns, though, are involuntary. They occur due to overload, excessive sensory input, emotional stress, or confusion. When a meltdown occurs, your child's nervous system is overwhelmed and they can't just "snap out of it." Reasoning, negotiating, or distractions don't help because their brain has entered survival mode; fight, flight, or freeze takes over. Stress hormones flood their body, their heart races, muscles tighten, and logic goes out the window. In this state, your child isn't trying to manipulate; they're trying to endure an experience that feels out of control.

If your child is denied ice cream in a store and screams, checking your face for a reaction, that's likely a tantrum. If you remain firm or offer comfort but don't give in, the tantrum fades since the behavior is strategic, though it hardly feels that way in the moment.

Contrast that with a meltdown in the same store: your child screams after the loudspeaker blares or the lights flicker too brightly. There's no demand, just distress rising until it bursts. You try to help, but your child might not respond, accept comfort, or communicate. Recovery takes time and your child may seem drained or confused afterward.

Visual Comparison Chart: Meltdowns vs. Tantrums

- Feature Meltdown Tantrum Trigger Overload (sensory, emotional, cognitive)
- Goal not met (wants something)
- Voluntary? Involuntary – not under child's control Voluntary – goal-driven Behavior
- Lose speech; intense crying; shutdown
- Crying; yelling; watching adult
- Stops if…Overload subsides; time & support
- Goal achieved/ignored long enough
- Recovery Slow; exhaustion common
- Quick once goal is met/ignored

Even when you understand this distinction, you might second-guess yourself, especially faced with comments like, "She just wants attention," or "He's manipulating you." But during a true meltdown, relief, not attention, is the goal. Your child needs understanding and support. Recognizing this reduces feelings of blame or frustration and encourages a compassionate response.

During meltdowns, your child's brain is attempting to protect them from overwhelming sensations or emotions. They are not being bad or stubborn; they're in distress and need help to calm down. Sometimes, this means removing triggers; other times, it means staying near while they ride out the storm. No amount of discipline or logic will halt a meltdown in its tracks.

You can't always prevent meltdowns, but you can get better at spotting early signs: clenched hands, tense face, pacing or repetitive motions. These are signals that stress is building. If you catch them early, you can offer a break or relocate to a quieter area before things escalate.

Remember: your child isn't acting out to get attention or embarrass you. Their body and mind are overwhelmed and sounding an alarm. Even if others judge or don't understand, trust your instincts; you know your child best. Respond with empathy.

Real-Life Scenario Reflection

Recall a tough public moment with your child. How did you feel? What triggered your childhood, hunger, crowds? Did you see any warning signs? Think about what helped, even a little. Write down three words describing your feelings as it happened. This isn't to assign blame; it's to help you spot patterns and build confidence for next time.

Meltdowns are signals that help is needed now, not failures. As you get better at recognizing what's beneath the surface and differentiating meltdowns from tantrums, you can respond with more compassion to your child and yourself.

Sensory Triggers—Building a Personalized Sensory Profile

Every child's body is a finely tuned sensory system, and for autistic kids, certain sights, sounds, or textures can tip the scales from calm to chaos in a matter of seconds. You may notice your child covering their ears at the hum of a blender, bolting from fluorescent lights at the store, or recoiling from the feel of scratchy socks. Sometimes, these reactions seem random or even contradictory. One day, hugs are soothing: the next, they're unbearable. Learning to identify these sensory triggers can help you approach meltdowns more effectively and reduce stress for everyone involved. I always encourage parents to start with careful observation.

Keep a small notebook or use your phone's notes app to create a "sensory diary." Each time your child struggles or lights up with joy, jot down what's happening around them. Focus on the environment: Are there loud noises? Bright or flickering lights? Unusual smells? What is your child wearing? Did someone touch them unexpectedly? Over time, patterns emerge that reveal which sensory inputs lead to overload and which bring comfort.

The human body processes sensory input through several systems, some more obvious than others. Auditory triggers include loud sounds, echoing rooms, or even background chatter that most people tune out. Visual triggers can be glaring lights, cluttered spaces, or fast-moving crowds. Tactile sensitivity is common, characterized by experiences such as itchy tags, sticky hands, hair brushing, or sudden hugs. Some children are sensitive to olfactory input: strong perfumes, cleaning products, or the scent of certain foods can trigger agitation. Then there's proprioception and vestibular input, these relate to movement and body awareness. Kids might crave bouncing, spinning, or deep squeezes (proprioception) or become dizzy and disoriented by gentle rocking (vestibular). It's not unusual for a child to seek out one kind of sensation while fiercely avoiding another. For example, a child might love the weight of a heavy blanket but hate the feel of light touch on their arm.

Building a sensory profile isn't just about noticing what goes wrong; it's also about discovering what feels good for your child. Involve your child in this process as much as possible, even young kids can point to pictures or choose "happy" or "no thank you" faces for different sensations. You might ask them to rate activities or environments using thumbs up/down, colored stickers, or simple drawings of smiley/sad faces. Over a week or two, fill out a checklist: Which clothes are favorites? Which foods get spat out? Where do meltdowns seem more likely, noisy restaurants, crowded playgrounds, bright shops? Which activities soothe: swinging, squeezing playdough, listening to music? Pay close attention to subtle clues—does your child chew their shirt when overwhelmed or seek out cold drinks after stressful days?

Sensory triggers aren't always straightforward. Sometimes a meltdown seems to come from nowhere because the trigger is cumulative; small annoyances build until your child's threshold is crossed. Or the same sensation can be both a comfort and a stressor. Depending on the context, your child might crave deep hugs at home but flinch away from a friend's gentle pat at school. If you're struggling to pinpoint causes, try looking for patterns over several days: Does roughhousing before dinner help with sitting at the table, or does it make things worse? Does scent-free laundry detergent help with dressing battles? Do sunglasses lower anxiety in bright spaces? When you hit on a mystery, say your child loves pressure but not brushing, note it without judgment; these mixed responses are common and valid.

Sensory Diary Template

Date/Time Location

What happened before meltdown (or happy moment)?

Sounds Lights Smells Touch Movement

Clothes/Fabrics Food/Drink

My child's reaction (body language, words)

Comfort strategies tried

What helped?

Example: 2 pm Saturday

Grocery store checkout, Waiting in line; lots of people talking

Loud PA system

Bright lights overhead

Smell of coffee nearby

Bumped by cart

Standing still Sweater (itchy)

None Covered ears, stomped foot, started crying

Offered headphones, held hand, left store early

Headphones helped a little; leaving helped most

Working together with your child to create this profile not only gives you practical data, but it also empowers your child to recognize and advocate for their own needs over time. You'll probably discover both "favorites" (soft fleece blankets, swinging on playgrounds) and "avoids" (tags in shirts, hand dryers in public toilets). Use this information to modify environments when possible and prepare for unavoidable triggers with calming strategies at hand. If you ever feel stuck or unsure, maybe responses are wildly inconsistent; remind yourself that sensory processing isn't always logical. Allow flexibility and keep updating your profile as your child grows and changes. This process isn't about eliminating every challenge but about understanding your child's unique sensory landscape so you can support them with calm confidence each day.

The Calming Toolkit—Weighted Items, Fidgets, and Sensory Diets

Life with an autistic child is often unpredictable and full of hidden challenges. A "calming toolkit" can be a lifesaver, whether at home or on the go. This toolkit isn't generic, but is personalized with sensory supports tailored to your child's preferences and sensitivities. Packed in a backpack or tote, it's your go-to for challenging moments, in waiting rooms, traffic, or busy family gatherings.

Build your toolkit with a checklist of your child's favorites. For kids who crave deep pressure, include a small weighted lap pad or compression vest. For those who need to keep their hands busy, pack fidget toys, squishy balls, putty, or spinners. If your child self-soothes by chewing, add chewable jewelry. Noise-canceling headphones are essential for sound-sensitive children, while sunglasses or a cap help with bothersome lighting. Comfort objects, such as a familiar blanket or stuffed animal, can be grounding in new places. Always add snacks and a water bottle, since hunger and thirst can make regulation harder. The key is to adapt the kit to your child's sensory profile and update it as their needs change.

Weighted Items

Weighted blankets, vests, and lap pads provide deep pressure, which can calm the nervous system and help your child feel safe. This sensation often feels grounding, like a warm hug. Use these tools carefully, limit initial use to 10–20 minutes, supervise your child, and never use more than about 10% of your child's weight. Let your child decide when and how to use them; forcing can cause distress. Some prefer a compression vest under clothes at school; others like a weighted blanket for car rides or downtime. If you're trying weighted supports for the first time, consider borrowing one before buying to see how your child reacts, and adjust the support based on their response.

Fidgets, Chewelry, and Headphones

Fidget tools come in many styles. The best ones cater to your child's sensory needs. Some prefer resistance (putty), repetitive motion (spinners), or soft textures (fabric swatches). Fidgets help calm restless hands, allowing your child to focus or relax. Chewelry is perfect for oral seekers who chew on collars or pencils. Noise-canceling headphones block disruptive sounds, empowering your child to manage noisy environments. Your child can choose when to use them for a sense of control.

Keeping the Toolkit Dynamic

Review and update your toolkit regularly. Children's preferences change, so rotate items and involve your child in the packing process. Label everything sent to school to prevent loss and explain the items to teachers or caregivers.

The Sensory Diet: Regulation Throughout the Day

A toolkit helps in emergencies, but a proactive "sensory diet" keeps your child regulated on a regular basis. A sensory diet is a daily plan of activities that offers steady doses of sensory input to meet your child's needs and prevent sensory overload. For example, start mornings with trampoline time, have playdough after lunch, and end with rocking or swinging before bed. For movement seekers, schedule frequent outdoor breaks; for deep-pressure lovers, offer time under a heavy blanket after school. Activities like blowing bubbles or jumping jacks between tasks can also help with focus.

Trial and error is part of the process. Note which activities help and which don't. Build sensory breaks into transitions by dimming lights before meals, observing quiet time after outings, or playing soft music during baths. Share your sensory diet with teachers so they can support your child's regulation at school as well. The aim isn't perfection, but consistent support to help your child feel more regulated and less prone to meltdowns.

Having these tools and routines shifts daily life in your favor. Whether it's a fidget spinner during errands or the calming weight of a lap pad at school, these supports aren't "crutches", they're bridges, helping your child feel safe and capable in a world not designed for their needs.

Public Meltdowns—Quick-Reference Flowcharts for Crisis Moments

When a meltdown erupts in public, it can feel like you're on stage without a script, with everyone watching and the pressure building quickly. Instead of scrambling in survival mode, imagine a mental flowchart: specific, steady steps for stability. Begin by reading your child's body language. If agitation is rising, check the environment; loud, crowded, or bright spaces can heighten distress. If possible, move to a quieter area or shield your child by positioning yourself between them and the crowd, creating a small protective bubble. Offer ear defenders or a comfort item if available. Sometimes, just getting down to your child's level can reduce the intensity for both of you.

If the meltdown occurs before you can adjust the setting, prioritize containment over control. First, prioritize safety, remove nearby hazards, or shift away from crowds or traffic. Try not to let bystanders' reactions affect you; your child's well-being should always come first. Keep your tone calm and low, even if you're anxious. Use practiced scripts if you have them: "It's okay. I'm here." Avoid rapid questions or long reasoning, as your child can't process much language in the heat of a meltdown.

When the storm passes, support recovery step by step. Offer water or a favorite snack. Give your child a bit of space if needed, but don't drift far unless they want to be alone. If you need to abandon plans, leaving a cart behind or skipping a meal out, do it without apology. Changing plans isn't failure, it's adapting bravely. Your dignity and your child's sense of safety are more important than sticking to a schedule.

Quick-Reference Flowchart: Before, During, After

Before Meltdown:

- Watch for warning signs (tensing up, covering ears, rapid breathing)
- Move toward a quieter, less busy spot
- Offer something calming (ear defenders, fidget toy, snack)
- Use brief scripts: "It's loud. Let's sit here."

During Meltdown:

- Ensure safety (remove hazards, shield from crowds)
- Stay close but don't force contact
- Speak softly: "You're safe. I'm not leaving."
- Ignore other people; focus on your child

After Meltdown:

- Offer water or a snack
- Use comforting routines ("Want your blanket?")

- Debrief gently when calm: "That was rough. Ready to go home?"
- Allow yourself to end the outing

Bringing a public meltdown emergency kit provides relief. Have ear defenders handy; they're lightweight and can block noise from stores or sirens. A comfort object, whether a toy, fabric, or a weighted stone, quickly reassures. Carry a laminated card: "My child is autistic and may need space or extra time. Thank you for understanding." This card isn't only for others but also eases your burden by minimizing the need to explain in stressful moments.

Scripts are invaluable when strangers comment or give advice. You owe no one an explanation, but it's helpful to have ready responses for staff or passersby: "My child is autistic and needs a few minutes. I appreciate your patience," or "We're having a hard moment. Thank you for understanding." If someone intervenes or judges, stand firm: "We're handling it—thanks for giving us space." Some days, you might want to educate, while other days, you'll want to leave quickly.

Never hesitate to drop everything and leave if it's what your child needs. Abandoning groceries, hurriedly exiting a gathering, or leaving personal belongings isn't being flaky, it's fierce advocacy. Protecting your child's dignity and sense of safety matters far more than appearances or outside expectations. Sometimes, just stepping outside can reset both of you.

You know your child better than anyone else around you. You're allowed to protect their peace and your own, even if it looks messy or misunderstood from the outside. With practice, these steps will feel more automatic, grounded in confidence rather than panic, even if passersby don't understand.

After the Storm—Repairing Connection and Rebuilding Safety

When the chaos of a meltdown finally ebbs, you and your child may both feel wrung out. There's a strange hush, a kind of emotional hangover, where relief and worry mingle. This is the moment to rebuild what got shaken gently. Your first instinct might be to analyze or fix, but what matters most now is restoring a sense of safety and trust. You don't have to say much. Sometimes the softest words are the most powerful: "That was hard. I'm right here." Sit beside your child or, if they're open, offer a gentle touch or just your quiet presence. The goal isn't to interrogate or explain but to let your child know nothing they did has changed how you feel about them.

Debriefing with your child works best when you keep it simple, honest, and free of blame. Use language that describes, not judges: "You were really upset earlier. Are you okay now? Is there anything you want or need?" Some children may not respond with words, and that's okay. You can ask if they want to draw, squeeze your hand, or choose a favorite calming activity. If your child uses visuals, offer them options: pictures of a quiet room, a glass of water, or their weighted blanket. Even just acknowledging what happened, "That was a big feeling", can make your child feel seen and safe.

After meltdowns, many kids crave routine and comfort. Reset rituals can be simple but powerful. Dim the lights and tuck yourselves under a soft blanket. Maybe you play gentle music, rock side by side in a chair, or watch the ceiling fan together for a few minutes. Some children find peace in their sensory corner or curled up with a stuffed animal. Others need space before they can come close again. Let your child set the pace and choose what feels best. Sometimes it's a shared snack, a warm bath, or even silence together on the couch while everyone's heartbeat slows.

As much as your child needs reassurance, so do you. Meltdowns can leave parents feeling shaken, helpless, even angry or ashamed. Those feelings are real; acknowledge them without guilt. Take a few deep breaths. Stand by an open window or step outside for fresh air if possible. If your hands are trembling, let them rest on your chest and focus on taking slow, deep breaths. Even two minutes of mindful breathing can help calm your nervous system back from a state of high alert. Later, jot down a note in your phone or on a scrap of paper about what helped and what didn't. Just a few words will do. "Headphones worked," "Needed more time before going back in," "Felt judged but kept calm." This private reflection helps you spot patterns over time and reminds you that you're learning too.

Every meltdown carves out an opportunity to build resilience in both you and your child. When everyone is calm again, think together about what could help next time. With older kids or those who use visuals, you might ask: "If you feel upset again, could you show me your break card sooner?" Or, "Would it help if we brought your headphones next time?" If your child shrugs or resists talking about it, don't push; sometimes simply knowing they have choices for next time makes all the difference.

Encourage small steps toward self-advocacy without putting pressure on them. Perhaps your child will point to their water bottle when feeling overwhelmed next time or use a gesture to indicate "stop." Celebrate these tiny victories; they're seeds for future problem-solving. When you review what happened with kindness rather than blame, you teach your child that big feelings are survivable and repair is always possible.

After meltdowns, remember that your needs matter too. Reach out to a friend or support group if you need to vent. Sometimes, just hearing "me too" from another parent can lighten the invisible load. If you keep a journal, write down not just the complex parts but also anything that went right: "Stayed patient," "Child let me sit nearby," "We recovered faster." These notes are proof of growth, especially on days when everything feels raw.

Meltdowns will never be easy to witness or manage, but every time you help your child through one with empathy and care, you're teaching something lasting: emotions can be wild but don't have to be feared, and connection always comes first.

Preventing Overwhelm—Micro-Routines and Transition Strategies

Preventing overwhelm often starts with micro-routines, tiny, reliable steps that help manage daily chaos. When life feels unpredictable, these small routines create islands of calm for your child. For example, breaking down "getting ready to leave" into simple steps, such as putting on shoes, grabbing the backpack, putting on a coat, opening the door, each with a corresponding visual card, replaces rushing or following orders with a predictable structure. This minimizes anxiety and gives your child a sense of control. The same approach applies to older kids; concise routines for things like brushing teeth or prepping homework reduce stress and conflict for everyone.

Lengthy activities can be draining, so build in mini-breaks, just two minutes to jump, squeeze a fidget, or sip water, before overwhelm hits. These aren't rewards but part of the day's rhythm, helping your child pace themselves. When these pauses are expected, children don't feel pressured to "hold it together" endlessly, and you can spot early signs of stress before they escalate.

Transitions are another typical challenge; even moving between enjoyable activities can prompt anxiety or resistance. Giving advance warnings helps: a visual or audio five-minute timer signals change is coming, so nothing is a surprise. For example, saying, "Five more minutes, then we clean up," while showing a timer often prevents protests.

Transition objects, like a favorite toy, card, or stone, can also help. Carrying this familiar item between activities offers comfort and reinforces that while things change, something reassuring comes along. Children may use their object when moving between rooms, leaving the house, or running errands, a small gesture that can ease transitions.

Incorporate planned downtime and sensory breaks, just as you schedule meals or bedtime. If you know that school or therapy will challenge your child, reserve post-activity quiet time for them to decompress. This might be listening to music alone, lying under a weighted blanket, or quietly building with blocks. You don't need hours; even fifteen minutes can help your child recharge and prevent minor frustrations from escalating.

Of course, routines sometimes fall apart, the bus is late, a favorite shirt isn't clean, or you get stuck in traffic. Flexibility is key, and visual "Plan B" charts help your child see what happens if plans change: if playground time is cancelled, maybe there's a dance break or an early snack. Previewing alternatives ahead of time reduces panic and surprise when reality shifts.

Social stories are another support for sudden changes. Simple picture-based sentences can explain what's happening and what comes next: "Today the store was closed. We will go tomorrow instead." Reading these together prepares your child for change as part of life, showing there's always a next step even when things don't work out.

The beauty of micro-routines and planned transitions is how they invite your child to actively participate in daily life. These tools provide structure but also space for your child's personality; they might choose the next routine card or change their transition object each week.

Pay attention to what works and be ready to adjust if something doesn't. Flexibility means adapting without losing all routine, bending but not breaking when unexpected things happen. Over time, these habits make your days smoother and keep your reactions calmer, even when plans go awry.

Short moments of predictability and gentle preparation can make each day feel safer and more manageable. These routines act as scaffolding, not cages: they support your child's growth and independence while helping prevent overwhelm.

Sometimes the smallest adjustments, a picture card, a gentle warning, a quick, quiet break, bring the greatest relief. Layering these routines and transition supports throughout your day creates a more predictable, reassuring world for your child. This foundation helps your child feel understood and ready, enabling you both to handle new challenges with greater confidence. The next chapter will focus on nurturing independence, so your child can tackle new goals step by step and you can celebrate every achievement together.

Chapter 5:
Daily Life, Simplified—Building Routines That Work for Your Family

Morning Routines—Visual Schedules and "First-Then" Boards

Weekday mornings with an autistic child can be uniquely chaotic; minor changes or disruptions often trigger a series of issues, from refusing to get out of bed to needing to line up toys before putting on shoes. These seemingly small details affect the entire family's day. If you're looking for ways to create calmer, more predictable mornings, you're not alone. One of the most effective strategies is using visual schedules and "first-then" boards.

A visual morning schedule isn't about rigid rules, but rather about giving children clear, easy-to-understand steps they can see. Break the morning into specific actions: wake up, use the bathroom, get dressed, eat breakfast, gather backpack, put on shoes, and leave. For many autistic children, visual cues (such as photos or icons) are less overwhelming than spoken instructions. Start by identifying which transitions cause trouble (such as changing clothes or eating breakfast) and add extra support to those steps in your schedule.

Create the schedule using images meaningful to your child, photos you take (their toothbrush, their cereal, their shoes) or simple colorful icons from the internet. Laminate them or use plastic sleeves for durability. Arrange the steps in a row, column, or on a magnetic board. Select what suits your space and your child's learning style. Many parents favor Velcro strips so kids can peel off finished steps, or a flipbook/digital app where tasks disappear with a tap. The crucial part is keeping the schedule interactive and at your child's eye level.

Introduce the visual schedule before the morning rush. Walk through it together, previewing the steps with "First we do this, then that," and let your child practice moving or flipping the icons. For kids who need extra motivation or struggle with transitions, "first-then" boards are helpful. These show just two steps: what happens now and what's next ("First brush teeth, then iPad time"; "First get dressed, then music"). This clear cause-and-effect pairing helps kids understand that effort brings reward, increasing motivation and building trust. Keep the board handy during tough transitions and swap out icons as needed.

Expect some challenges, such as slow transitions, reluctance to move on, or upset over unexpected changes. Try adding a game-like element: set a kitchen timer or use a fun-sound app, and challenge your child to finish a step before time's up. Praise them for effort and participation—"You pressed the toothpaste before the beep! High five!" If your child gets stuck, break down the steps further or use more detailed images (separate icons for "shirt," "pants," and "socks" rather than just "get dressed"). Allowing choices within the routine ("Brush teeth before or after breakfast?") can also help, giving your child a sense of control.

Involving your child in building and adjusting the schedule is a powerful approach. Let them choose task pictures, pose for photos, or decorate the board with favorite stickers. If they love trains, use related stickers or a train-shaped timer. Have a brief weekly review together, perhaps on Sunday night, asking what's working and what needs to change. Perhaps they would like to swap the order of steps or prefer a different image. These tweaks give your child ownership of the morning routine, making it more collaborative and less mandatory.

Visual Routine Builder—Quick Exercise

Spend fifteen minutes with your child to build the next morning's schedule. Gather or snap photos/icons for each step and let your child help choose them. Arrange them in a row on cardboard or use a digital app. Walk through each step now, so they feel familiar the next day. Ask your child if they would like to add anything (such as a sticker for each task completed or a special icon for their favorite breakfast). Put the schedule where your child will see it first thing in the morning.

Although building visual routines may take effort initially, it quickly leads to smoother mornings and fewer battles over each small step. With practice and minor tweaks based on your child's feedback, these routines help transform chaotic mornings into something much more manageable, even when other things go awry.

Mealtime Solutions—Handling Picky Eating and Food Aversions

Mealtimes can feel like an uphill climb for many families raising autistic children. You might spend an hour cooking, only to have your child refuse even a taste, or melt down at the sight of "the wrong" sauce on their plate. If you're exhausted by food battles, you're not alone. Picky eating in autistic kids isn't just stubbornness; it's a tangled mix of sensory sensitivities, routines, and sometimes anxiety around change. Food refusal often starts with the way something feels, smells, or looks rather than taste alone. Some children gag at mushy textures or only tolerate crunchy foods. Others reject foods that are mixed together or refuse anything of a specific color. Even the sound of a fork scraping a plate or the smell of cooking can overwhelm.

Understanding what's behind your child's refusal helps you choose effective strategies. I encourage parents to use a sensory checklist to spot patterns. Notice if your child avoids foods that are wet or sticky, objects to bright colors (like orange carrots), or reacts to strong smells. Keep a simple log for a week, jotting down reactions, not just what your child eats, but what gets pushed away or triggers distress. Does temperature matter? Many kids will only eat food that's cold or at room temperature. For others, the look of mixed textures, such as stew with vegetables floating in broth- makes a dish unappetizing.

Once you know the triggers, you can slowly help your child become more comfortable around new foods using stepwise desensitization.

Think of it as building a ladder: the first rung is simply allowing the new food to be present at the table. No pressure to eat, just look at it. When your child is ready, move on to touching the food with a fork or finger, then smelling it, and possibly giving a gentle poke. The next goal is to hold it near the mouth or lick it. Only after several successful steps would you encourage an actual bite. This process, sometimes called a "food exposure hierarchy"- works best when you celebrate every step, not just eating. For some kids, progress is slow, but these tiny victories matter.

Food chaining can also help if your child will only eat certain brands or types of food. This method begins with a preferred food and introduces gradual changes, such as transitioning from chicken nuggets to homemade breaded chicken strips and then to plain baked chicken. Small tweaks in shape, brand, or preparation help children expand their comfort zone without dramatic leaps. Celebrate if your child moves from triangle-shaped toast to square toast; that's real progress.

Visual support reduces anxiety by making meals predictable and giving choices within boundaries. Prepare a simple visual menu board with photos or icons for each meal option, such as sandwiches, yogurt, and fruit slices. Before eating, let your child pick from two or three options using "choice cards." This approach offers autonomy and reduces power struggles over surprise foods. Some families set up a routine where the child helps set the table or loads their plate using their menu card choices.

Maintaining a peaceful mealtime atmosphere matters as much as the food itself. Try to avoid "food battles" where you plead for bites or threaten to take away dessert. Instead, adopt an "all foods fit" philosophy: all safe foods are welcome at the table, and no food is labeled as "bad" or "forbidden." If your child only eats crackers and applesauce one night, that's okay, you can offer variety again tomorrow. Keep the portions small and pressure low.

Positive reinforcement is key. Praise trying and exploring, not just swallowing. Acknowledge non-eating steps: "You touched the carrot!

That's brave." You could use sticker charts for each step up the hierarchy or special tokens for exploring a new food but keep rewards simple and low-pressure. Avoid bribing with dessert for finishing all bites; this can backfire and increase stress.

Family dynamics can make picky eating even trickier. Siblings may complain about "baby rules," or other adults might judge your approach. Hold firm to your plan and explain you're working toward comfort and confidence around food, not quick fixes. Make everyone's needs part of the discussion by rotating who chooses a side dish or allowing siblings to help with serving.

If mealtimes remain stressful after trying these strategies, consider reaching out to an occupational therapist or feeding specialist who is familiar with autism and sensory processing. Sometimes professional support is necessary for more severe aversions or anxiety around eating.

Mealtime success doesn't mean getting your child to eat everything on their plate right away. It means creating an environment where your child feels safe to explore and try at their own pace. Even if progress seems slow and incremental, every small step forward is worth celebrating, for both your child and your family's peace of mind.

Sleep Support—Creating Calm Evenings and Predictable Bedtimes

Bedtime can be tough for families, especially when your child is sensitive to sensory input and routine changes. Resistance, negotiations, or night waking may leave you frustrated and exhausted. However, there are real, practical ways to create a calmer, more predictable bedtime, even if sleep has been a longstanding struggle.

Pay special attention to the hour leading up to bedtime. This is a crucial time for your child's body and mind to slow down. For autistic children, gradually reducing stimulation can be extremely helpful. Start by dimming lights to signal nighttime, and lower the screen and background noise volume, including TV, music, and household chatter.

Many parents opt for softer lighting or blackout curtains to ease into bedtime, especially during long summer evenings. Introducing quiet activities after dinner, such as puzzles, coloring, gentle music, or cuddling with stuffed animals, can further help settle your child. Avoid screens in this final hour, if possible, as their light can make it more difficult to fall asleep.

A visual bedtime routine can eliminate guesswork and soothe anxiety about what's next. Use simple photos or drawings to illustrate each step, such as bath time, pajamas, tooth brushing, story time, cuddles, and lights out. Lay these out in a row by the bed or on a clipboard that your child can hold. Go through the routine together at first, naming each step as you go. In time, your child will anticipate the sequence, making bedtime smoother. For extra preparation, consider social stories: picture books that explain bedtime routines and help make them familiar.

Even with a routine, some nights will be harder than others. Many children struggle to relax, wake up frequently, or rise very early. Evidence-based strategies can help: weighted blankets or compression sheets provide calming, deep pressure, while background white noise, such as a fan or machine, can muffle sudden household sounds. A "sleep box" with special items (favorite book, soft toy, lavender sachet, or stress ball) used only at bedtime helps cue sleep. Introduce the box just before bed, so your child associates its contents with getting ready to sleep.

Prioritize keeping the bedtime routine steady, but stay flexible for life's disruptions, such as illness, travel, or overnight visits. Prepare a "sleep on the go" kit: favorite pillowcase, backup pajamas, sleep box items, and a copy of the visual routine. When away from home, keep the sequence of steps consistent. Use photos or icons to remind your child what's next and calmly discuss any changes ahead of time.

You'll have nights where nothing works, your child may be wide awake at midnight or upset by a bad dream. In these moments, respond predictably and calmly: gently guide them back to bed using as few words as possible. Routine reminders ("It's still bedtime; here's your bear") are usually more effective than lengthy explanations. For early waking, blackout curtains help block dawn light, and a simple digital clock with color cues can show when it's truly time to get up.

Some sleep problems, like ongoing insomnia, night terrors, or extreme early rising, persist despite routine and environmental shifts. In these cases, consult a pediatrician or sleep specialist experienced with autism; sometimes professional support is necessary alongside home strategies.

Not every night will be perfect, but predictable evenings and routines help your child's body and mind unwind. Over time, with patience and small tweaks, you'll find patterns that support your family's needs and hopefully bring back a bit of evening peace.

Bedtime Routine Reflection

After your child settles, take five minutes to jot down what worked and what didn't in your bedtime routine. Identify steps that caused stress or parts that seemed to comfort your child. Use these quick notes to adjust tomorrow's approach, like swapping a visual cue or adding a calming item to the sleep box. Small daily changes can make a big difference as you refine your family's routine.

Getting Out the Door—Transition Routines for School and Outings

Leaving the house on time can feel like a high-stakes mission. A small setback can lead to running late, your child melting down, and both of you feeling on edge before the day starts. For many families, transitions, like getting to school or appointments, are the toughest parts of the routine. The key is to break these moments into clear, manageable steps and plan for disruptions before they happen. Establish a step-by-step routine you follow each time you leave. Give an early heads-up with a simple cue: "Five more minutes until we go." Use a visual and auditory countdown timer, like your phone, a kitchen timer, or a sand timer, to signal that time is almost up. This warning isn't just about being punctual; it's about helping your child shift gears at a pace they can handle. Some kids benefit from two warnings: perhaps a ten-minute reminder, then the five-minute countdown with the timer for the final stretch.

As time winds down, narrate the process out loud: "In two minutes, we'll put on shoes and get your backpack." Walk through each step: "First shoes, then coat, then we'll open the door." Visual cues can help; a mini-schedule by the door with pictures or icons for each step. For children who forget or stall, point to each item on the list as you go. Some families use a basket or tray for shoes, a backpack, or other essentials, serving as a visual checklist.

A "go bag" can smooth transitions. Pack it ahead of time with sensory tools and comfort items tailored to your child's needs: noise-canceling headphones for loud spaces, a favorite fidget or chew toy, a mess-free snack, and a laminated copy of your visual schedule. Include wipes, an extra shirt, and any needed medications. Having this bag ready avoids last-minute scrambling and provides a sense of security in new or unpredictable settings.

For unfamiliar outings, such as the first day at a new school, doctor's office, or playground, previewing the environment can help ease anxiety. Use your phone to create a photo book, capturing the building, entryway, classroom, waiting rooms, and the faces of staff members, if possible. Review these together with your child before the visit. If you can, do a practice run while it's quiet, drive by the school or visit the clinic lobby. This helps transform unfamiliar places into something more predictable and less intimidating.

Social stories also help children prepare for transitions, such as riding the bus or visiting a new store. Create a simple sequence with photos or drawings: "First, we ride the bus. There will be other people. The driver says hello. We sit in our seats and look out the window." Keep language short and concrete. Read these stories before and on the day of the outing, if needed.

Even with planning, last-minute changes can occur, such as rain canceling a park trip or an appointment getting rescheduled. These changes are particularly challenging for any child, especially those who require predictability. "Plan B" visuals help. Use a Velcro-backed "change" icon on your schedule; when plans shift, swap in the next step or attach the "change" icon to signal something unexpected. Use calm, simple language: "Change of plan, we're not going to the dentist today. We'll go another time. Now we'll have playground time instead."

Some children need more concrete cues to accept changes, a special "plan B" card they can hold, or a familiar comfort item when plans shift. Remind them that while plans might change, some things remain steady: "You still have your blue headphones and snack." If you can, let your child choose between two backup options ("We can't go to the pool, but do you want ice cream or to play at home?"). This restores some sense of control.

Practice makes transition routines easier: pack bags the night before, talk through steps aloud, and preview new places. The more you repeat these routines, the more confident you and your child will become on busy mornings or during surprise outings. Over time, these transition tools become second nature. With less chaos at the door, everyone starts the day a little calmer, even if socks still sometimes end up backwards.

Chore Time—Teaching Life Skills Through Play and Predictability

Teaching chores to autistic children is more than about keeping the house tidy; it's about building independence, boosting confidence, and giving your child a sense of pride in their own abilities. The trick is to think of chores not as one big demand, but as a collection of small, manageable actions. Many children find the phrase "clean your room" overwhelming, but breaking it down into steps can transform resistance into success. Begin by creating a task breakdown chart for each chore. For example, "brush teeth" becomes four simple steps: get the toothbrush, put on toothpaste, brush, then rinse. Use photos or drawings for each part, and place the chart at eye level in the bathroom or wherever the task happens. This kind of visual support turns chores into something concrete rather than a vague command.

For many families, weaving playfulness into chores brings relief and results. Children who resist folding laundry may light up at a "laundry race." Turn matching socks into a game: set a timer and see how many pairs you can find together before the buzzer. Or create a "laundry toss" with a basket across the room. Music is another powerful motivator. Choose a favorite song for toy cleanup and challenge everyone to beat the chorus. For kids who love cars or dinosaurs, use those interests as a hook. "Can you drive the cars into the 'garage' bin?" "Let's stomp like dinosaurs to put blocks away." When chores are part of a story or a game, kids are more likely to engage without protesting.

Routine is crucial for teaching life skills. Set a regular time for chores, maybe right after snack or before screen time, so your child knows what to expect. Using checklists eliminates the guesswork about what needs to be done. A simple checklist on the fridge or wall allows your child to check off tasks as they go. For younger kids or those who benefit from visual prompts, use pictures alongside words. Celebrate each completed step with enthusiastic praise, a high five, or a sticker on a chart. When your child sees their progress grow over the week, it feels more like an achievement than an obligation. Some families offer small rewards for filling out a sticker chart, reading an extra bedtime story, choosing dinner one night, or spending special time with a parent.

Family participation can make chore time something everyone looks forward to instead of dreads. Assigning roles helps each child understand what is expected and ensures fairness. Rotate the "helper of the day" title so each child gets a turn feeling special and in charge of certain tasks, maybe one child feeds the pet while another waters plants. For bigger chores, create "chore buddies." Pair up siblings or an adult and a child to tackle tasks together. This teamwork not only lightens the load but also gives opportunities for siblings to build positive bonds, especially important if jealousy or rivalry sometimes creeps in.

Adapting tasks for different ability levels ensures everyone can participate meaningfully. If your child struggles with fine motor skills, give them jobs that fit, like sorting utensils into a tray instead of folding clothes. Use larger tools or built-up handles when possible. If attention is an issue, keep chores short and concrete; even putting away three toys counts as success. Adjust expectations based on your child's strengths and needs; there's no rule that chores must look one way to "count."

Sometimes, progress is slow, and frustration bubbles up. On tough days, scale back rather than push harder. Acknowledge effort: "You handed me the socks. Thanks for helping." If your child refuses, invite them to watch while you do the chore, narrating each step in simple language. Over time, curiosity often grows into participation.

To keep things fresh, let your child help choose new jobs or decorate chore charts with favorite stickers or colors. Involve them in problem-solving: ask what would make chores more fun or easier ("Shall we try using a timer today?"). When children feel some control over how chores happen, they're much more likely to buy in.

I've seen families turn chore time into surprising moments of connection and growth. The child who refuses to touch laundry may become the best at matching colors by week three; the sibling who groans about emptying the dishwasher ends up racing their brother to finish first; the parent who dreads another battle finds themselves singing along to silly cleanup songs with both kids by their side.

Teaching life skills through play and predictability isn't quick or always smooth, but it does build real confidence that carries over into every other part of the day. Each small step, a matched sock, a rinsed toothbrush, and toys back in their bin, becomes proof that your child is capable and valued in your family's daily life.

Adapting for Sensory Needs—Home Setups That Reduce Stress

When you live with a child who senses the world differently, every room in your home can either soothe or overwhelm. Often, you might not realize what's setting your child off: a buzzing light fixture, the scratch of a sofa, or a jumble of colors and clutter. The first step is an honest look around. Conduct a sensory audit of each space, not just for potential dangers, but also for stress points and comfort opportunities. Walk through your home as if you're seeing it through your child's eyes. In the living room, is there glare from the windows? Does the hum of appliances echo in the background? Is the bedroom filled with bright colors or patterns that might overstimulate? Make notes on what seems to trigger discomfort or lead to calm. Write down which spaces your child seeks out when upset and where they avoid going. This simple exercise can reveal patterns you might have missed.

Creating calming spaces doesn't require a renovation budget or fancy therapy equipment. Small changes go a long way. Pick one spot, a corner in the living room, a patch of floor near their bed—and turn it into a "cozy corner." Gather soft pillows, a beanbag, or a weighted blanket. Dim the lighting with fairy lights or a small lamp. Sometimes, even hanging a sheet from the ceiling to create a little nook gives your child a safe retreat when everything else feels chaotic. Use blackout curtains to block harsh sunlight in overstimulating rooms or switch to softer bulbs in lamps. Consider how sound travels, absorbs noise, curtains muffle echoes, and even rolled-up towels (door snakes) at the bottom of doors cut down disruptive hallway sounds.

You don't need special gadgets to build sensory tools that work. Everyday items are your allies. A plastic bin filled with rice, dried beans, or clean sand instantly becomes a sensory station. Hide small toys or spoons inside for children to dig out and discover. For children who crave tactile input, offer sponges, soft brushes, or squishy balls. For oral seekers, keep straws or chewable jewelry handy. You can make noise-dampening changes with what you already have, layer rugs on hardwood floors, hang thick curtains where outside noise seeps in, and use bookshelf walls to separate noisy play from quiet zones. Sometimes, even changing the fabric on couch cushions or adding soft throws tames scratchy sensations.

Organization matters much more than you might expect. When you visually organize spaces, you reduce your child's stress and boost their independence. Use clear bins or color-coded baskets for toys, one color for cars, another for blocks, and a third for dolls or plushies. Label drawers and cabinets with both simple pictures and words so your child knows exactly where things belong. This way, clean-up is less about nagging and more about matching photographs, which many children find satisfying. In the bathroom, picture labels on baskets can indicate where toothbrushes belong or which towel is assigned to each person. In the kitchen, tape a simple photo of a cup to the cabinet door holding cups; no more digging through drawers and getting frustrated.

As you organize, keep sensory needs in mind. If certain supplies (like playdough or finger paint) are overwhelming, store them in opaque bins so your child isn't visually triggered every time they walk by. Reserve a basket for fidgets, headphones, or chew toys in areas where your child spends lots of time. For kids who love routine, lay out clothes in labeled drawers ("shirts," "pants," "socks"), making getting dressed a visual sequence rather than an argument.

You may want to try a sensory audit worksheet, where you list each space in your home and note the sights, sounds, textures, and smells present, as well as how your child responds to them. Track when your child seems calmest and when they seem most agitated, after time in the cozy corner? Or after being near the kitchen at dinnertime? Use your notes to guide changes: add a lamp here, swap a rug there, move noisy appliances away from quiet play spaces.

Even small adjustments create waves of relief. You may notice fewer meltdowns after adding a soft blanket to the reading nook or see your child settle faster when their bedroom lighting is gentle and predictable.

Family life feels less frantic when the environment supports regulation instead of fighting against it. The goal isn't perfection, but progress, creating spaces that invite comfort and provide your child with tools for calming down on their own.

As we wrap up this chapter on daily routines and supportive setups, remember that making these changes isn't about chasing an ideal but about making daily life smoother for everyone at home. Step by step, as you adapt rooms and routines, you'll see your child become more confident and independent in their own space. Up next: building stronger partnerships with teachers and professionals so this sense of calm and structure follows your child beyond your front door.

Chapter 6:
Advocacy and Access—Navigating Schools, Therapies, and Community Life

Navigating the IEP Process—Scripts, Checklists, and Red Flags

You find yourself in a small room with professionals, some taking notes while others work on laptops. There's a flurry of jargon and hurried politeness. You know your child's needs but translating them into concrete supports or services feels daunting. The IEP process can seem mysterious, filled with acronyms, shifting deadlines, and many opinions. Ultimately, though, the IEP isn't just administrative paperwork; it's your child's primary support system at school and your leverage to ensure their challenges and strengths are addressed effectively.

The journey begins with a referral for an evaluation, either by you or a teacher, if you believe you or your child may need additional support. Afterward, the school has a set timeline (often 60 days or less) to complete evaluations, which may include speech, occupational therapy, and academic assessments based on specific concerns. When the evaluations finish, you'll be invited to a meeting to discuss results and determine if your child qualifies for special education. If so, an IEP is drafted to specify present performance, measurable goals, services, accommodations, and progress tracking. This initial plan is revisited at least once a year, but meetings can be called whenever new issues arise.

Being well-organized makes the process smoother. Keep a dedicated folder for all reports, emails, and school-related notes. Collect documentation before meetings: evaluations, therapy notes, home behavior logs, and any parent input forms. A prepared list of questions or concerns will help keep you focused and organized. Review any draft IEP you receive in advance and highlight any unclear or missing information.

IEP Milestone Checklist

- Referral submitted/requested (date)
- Parental consent signed (date)
- Evaluations completed (date)
- Eligibility meeting held (date)
- Draft IEP received/reviewed (date)
- Annual review scheduled (date)
- Updated documents collected (date)
- Parent input statement prepared (date)

When requesting evaluations or meetings, use direct, written language. For example: "Dear [Special Education Coordinator], I am requesting a comprehensive evaluation for my child due to communication and sensory concerns. Please confirm receipt and next steps." Or, for a meeting: "I am requesting an IEP meeting to discuss recent changes in my child's needs and review current supports. Please provide available dates."

Meetings can be intimidating, especially when they involve vague or technical language. Always ask for clarification: "Can you explain how this goal is measured?" or "How will this strategy support my child's sensory needs?" If you disagree: "I'm concerned this goal isn't specific enough. Can we make it more concrete?" or "I'd like more detail on occupational therapy's role during activity transitions."

Be alert for red flags in the IEP draft or meeting: Goals should be specific and measurable (e.g., "will use AAC device three times per day over five days"), not vague, such as "will improve communication." If needed accommodations such as "preferential seating," "visual schedules," or "extra transition time" are absent, address this. Also, input from relevant specialists (speech, OT, behavioral) should be reflected if their services are mentioned. If support is denied without a clear explanation, ask for written documentation.

You don't have to face meetings alone, bring a friend, advocate, or relative, even to take notes. Record meetings (with notice) if allowed. Prepare a parent statement ahead of time—describe what you see at home, your concerns, hopes for progress, and outcomes that matter most. Sharing this early in the meeting confirms your role and perspective, which is essential for effective collaboration.

Reflection Exercise: Your Parent Input Statement

Before your meeting, jot down:

- Your child's biggest strengths
- Challenges at home or in the community
- Most helpful goals for this year
- What supports have worked or failed before Bring these notes to focus.

The IEP process can indeed be overwhelming, but by staying organized, asking clear questions, and insisting on specificity, you can ensure that your child's needs are recognized and effectively supported, rather than being lost in paperwork or polite conversation.

Communicating with Teachers—Templates for Effective Home-School Notes

When your child spends hours at school, you want their teachers to see them as more than a checklist or a file. You want them to know the child who loves dinosaurs, the one who melts down with loud bells, the one who sometimes needs a snack before circle time. Establishing productive communication with teachers often begins with a simple introduction, a "Meet My Child" one-pager. This isn't a dry medical report but a living snapshot: favorite activities, triggers, comfort items, sensory sensitivities, and what helps when things get tough. Share this one-pager at the start of each year or when staff changes. Include a warm photo if you'd like and keep the language direct yet friendly. For example: "Hi, I'm Sam's mom. Sam loves trains, needs quiet after lunch, and uses a chewy necklace when anxious. He may not answer questions out loud but will point to choices on his board. A calm hand on his shoulder helps him reset."

Daily and weekly communication logs bridge the gap between home and school, facilitating effective communication between parents and educators. Relying on memory or rushed emails leaves too much to chance, especially if your child is nonverbal or struggles to relay details. A simple checklist log can make all the difference. Picture a grid with columns for mood (happy, tired, upset), meals eaten (all, some, none), activities enjoyed (circle time, art, playground), sensory needs (used headphones, needed break), and challenges (meltdown during music, covered ears at assembly). Teachers can tick off boxes or add quick notes in minutes. This system works well for busy classrooms, and no one expects essays. If possible, create a template that fits your child's day and share copies with teachers or aides. Some parents use color-coded stickers for quick feedback: green for good mornings, yellow for minor bumps, red for tough days.

Weekly logs delve deeper, ideal for tracking patterns over time or sharing significant wins and setbacks. Teachers might jot down new skills (tried AAC device!), social moments (played ball with Alex), or concerns (avoided lunchtime). At home, you can add notes about sleep changes, medication tweaks, or family events that might ripple into school life. These back-and-forth builds trust and helps everyone spot what's working and what isn't.

Sometimes you'll notice things at home that aren't obvious to staff. Maybe Mondays always start rough after a weekend routine shift. Or your child resists school shoes but wears boots without complaint. Reaching out doesn't have to be confrontational. Try: "I noticed Jamie seems anxious on Mondays. Could we look at ways to ease arrivals?" Or: "Lately, Maya's been tired in the afternoons, maybe a short movement break would help?" Frame requests as shared problem-solving rather than criticism. Teachers respond best when they feel respected and included in the brainstorming process.

Digital tools offer flexibility when paper logs don't fit your life. Apps like ClassDojo or Seesaw allow quick updates, photos, or stickers as feedback. For older children or tech-savvy teams, short video updates or voice memos offer nuance that checklists sometimes lack. A teacher might send a 30-second clip of your child building a tower, or you might reply with a video showing how you use visuals at home for brushing teeth routines. Even a quick photo of a finished meal can signal success.

If language or literacy is a barrier for you or staff, visuals help. Use emoji checklists (☺ 😐 ☹), print symbol cards for behaviors or moods ("hungry," "frustrated," "calm"), or snap photos of favorite foods and calming strategies for reference. Visuals cut across language gaps and save time.

When issues arise, missed supports, repeated challenges, it's tempting to let frustration take over. Try taking a breath and starting with curiosity: "I saw Ben came home upset three days this week, could we talk through what's happening before math?" If you need to request a change, state what you're seeing and invite ideas: "Recess seems hard lately, do you have strategies that have worked with other students?" If you disagree with an approach, focus on your child's needs: "Liam's noise-canceling headphones weren't available yesterday; he came home very dysregulated. Let's make sure they're always within reach."

Teachers juggle dozens of responsibilities, so keep your communication clear and concise. Bullet points work well:

- Slept poorly last night
- Ate only yogurt for breakfast
- Extra sensitive to noise today
- Will bring a chewy necklace

End notes with gratitude when possible ("Thank you for trying the new routine yesterday, it helped!"). If communication breaks down or you feel unheard, escalate the situation slowly but firmly. Request meetings in writing, document all exchanges, and remind staff that you're working toward the same goal: your child's success and comfort.

When parents and teachers are on the same page, literally and figuratively, children benefit from consistency and understanding across their day. Small efforts to share information can prevent big problems down the line and help your child feel truly seen in every space they enter.

Choosing Therapies—Speech, OT, DIR/Floor time, and Evidence-Based Alternatives

Choosing a therapy for your child can feel overwhelming, with every provider promising results. No single approach works for all; the most effective therapy matches your child's strengths and your family's needs. Here's a concise guide to commonly recommended therapies with support from both research and practical experience.

Speech therapy is often a first step, especially if your child struggles with language, questions, or social skills. Speech therapists do much more than teach words; they help kids communicate using pictures, devices, or gestures, build conversation skills, and interpret nonverbal cues. Some focus on articulation, others on AAC (augmentative and alternative communication) like picture boards, apps, or speech-generating devices. For nonverbal or minimally verbal children, or those scripting lines from shows, speech therapy can transform repetitive behaviors into meaningful communication. Good therapists also coach parents on ways to support communication at home, during meals, play, or everyday errands.

Occupational therapy (OT) helps children navigate daily life, working through sensory sensitivities like disliking certain clothes or food textures, and mastering self-care activities (dressing, brushing teeth, using utensils). OTs assess sensory influences on mood and focus, then create "sensory diets"—activities to help regulate energy and teach coping skills for stressful situations. They address fine motor challenges, such as writing or cutting, and may suggest adaptive tools. Effective OTs offer strategies you can use at home and in school, not just in the clinic.

Relationship-based therapies like DIR/Floor time and SCERTS offer alternatives to rigid, compliance-focused methods. DIR/Floor time (Developmental, Individual-differences, Relationship-based) follows your child's lead, building on their interests and skills with playful, connection-driven activities, rather than forcing scripted behaviors or eye contact. SCERTS (Social Communication, Emotional Regulation, and Transactional Support) focuses on communication, emotional management, and supports strengths by training both kids and adults to adjust their interactions for clearer understanding and better self-regulation. Both models prioritize honoring a child's autonomy and neurodiversity.

Choosing any therapy requires weighing more than just brochures. Use a decision worksheet to compare options. Consider: Does the therapist have experience with similar kids? Do they invite parent participation and explain their approach clearly? Are your child's boundaries respected? Are goals relevant to daily life, not just compliance? If providers struggle to answer or become defensive, take caution.

Decision Worksheet: Is This Therapy a Good Fit?

- Therapist has experience with kids like mine (yes/no)
- Parents can watch or join sessions (yes/no)
- Goals explained clearly (yes/no)
- Focuses on strengths and needs (yes/no)
- Shares data, adjusts plans as needed (yes/no)
- My child is comfortable in sessions (yes/no)

Setting clear, measurable goals shows progress over time, e.g., "Will use AAC to request a break three times per day" or "Will tolerate tooth brushing for two minutes with help." At the start, ask: "How are we involved?" "How is success measured?" "What if my child isn't progressing?" "Can we adjust strategies?" Revisit goals as circumstances change; new teachers, moving, or illness often require updates.

Incorporating therapy into daily routines maximizes progress and reduces burnout. Instead of extra appointments, integrate practice into your schedule, using speech devices at meals or games, practicing OT strategies at bath time or during dressing. Share helpful techniques with teachers and other caregivers to build team consistency.

Coordinating multiple therapists or specialists is easier with regular communication. Set up a weekly check-in, maybe by email or a shared document, so everyone updates progress and discusses next steps. A simple table works well:

- Provider / Goal / Progress This Week / Parent Notes / Next Steps

A simple home activity schedule makes therapy manageable and relevant. Pick and track one main goal per day, trying a new food at dinner with OT tips, practicing social turn-taking with games, etc. Log successes and challenges for easy pattern recognition and swift adjustments.

Trust your expertise. Therapies should complement your family's life, not control it. If something feels off or too rigid, advocate for changes. The best therapy nurtures your child's growth, and also supports your family's well-being, confidence, and connection.

Understanding ABA—Controversies, Consent, and Parent Decision-Making

Applied Behavior Analysis (ABA) is frequently discussed in autism support as a structured teaching approach rooted in behaviorism. It breaks skills into small steps, using repetition and positive reinforcement, praise, tokens, or other rewards, to encourage desired behaviors. Discrete Trial Training, with its one-skill-at-a-time focus, is common, as is intensive data collection to track progress. Many families find this structured, goal-driven framework reassuring.

However, ABA's history is complex. Originating in the 1960s, its early forms sought to make autistic children "indistinguishable" from neurotypical peers, sometimes through harsh measures. Today, most providers say they prioritize positive feedback and reject punitive methods, but reducing "problem behaviors" and teaching expected social skills through repetitive drills remain core features.

Despite being presented as the "gold standard" by many schools and doctors, ABA faces strong opposition, especially from autistic adults and neurodiversity advocates. Critics question whether compliance-based goals, like enforced eye contact, sitting still, or strict instruction-following, truly benefit children. Such goals can suppress natural self-regulation behaviors (stimming) and may make kids feel pressured to mask their true selves. Many autistic adults recall ABA as traumatic, describing feelings of being controlled or compelled to win approval by hiding who they are.

The debate has intensified in places like the UK, where neurodiversity advocates argue for therapies that value children's autonomy and emotional well-being, not just outward compliance. For many families, the core concern is whether therapy helps their child flourish as themselves or simply conform. Consent is central: Can your child say "no"? Are their preferences considered? Is there a focus on authentic connection, choice, and rest?

If you're evaluating ABA or facing pressure to enroll, ask direct questions about autonomy and respect. Some key areas to discuss with providers include:

- How do you include my child's interests and preferences?
- What if my child refuses a task—will you respect their "no"?
- Are stimming behaviors allowed?
- How is self-advocacy supported?
- How do you handle distress or resistance?
- Are physical prompts or restraints used?
- Who sets therapy goals, you, us, or my child?

These questions help determine whether the program prioritizes your child's autonomy or focuses solely on reshaping behavior.

You might feel pressured by schools or professionals insisting on ABA as the only valid approach. It's acceptable to express your family's comfort zones:

- "We want therapies that focus on communication and self-advocacy rather than compliance."
- "Can goals emphasize my child's comfort and strengths?"
- "We need a therapy plan with downtime and flexibility alongside structure."

If intensive hours or rigid approaches aren't working, request changes:

- "Could we add more breaks and sensory supports?"
- "Can we include more play-based learning instead of table work?"
- "We want refusals to be seen as communication, not problems to fix."

If a provider can't or won't adapt, it's appropriate to seek a better fit elsewhere.

Parents often feel conflicted, doubting strict approaches but fearing missed opportunities. Trust your instincts. There's no shame in changing course if a certain therapy doesn't feel right for your child. Opting out or adapting a therapy is not denial of opportunity; it's honoring your child's needs and your family's values.

A practical way to evaluate a therapy: Observe your child after each session. Are they happy, relaxed, and making progress that feels meaningful? Or are they anxious, withdrawn, or dreading therapy? Trust your observations. Good support should build your child's confidence and joy, not just enforce compliance.

Consent matters deeply. Children deserve to be heard, whether through words, gestures, or devices. Decisions about therapy should be grounded in respect for autonomy and emotional well-being. If you ever worry that your child's comfort is ignored in favor of "results," it's good to pause and reconsider.

Here are some conversation starters with professionals:

- "How does your approach support our child's comfort and communication over compliance?"
- "How do you value self-advocacy and choice in your therapy?"
- "Can we discuss how your goals align with our child's strengths and interests?"

You'll encounter both positive and negative stories about ABA. Gather information from a range of sources: autistic adults, other parents, and therapists open to partnership. Your choices can evolve as your child's needs and your understanding change.

Navigating therapy is not about winning debates with experts, but about securing safe, flexible, and genuinely respectful support for your child.

Accessing Funding and Community Resources—Grants, Medicaid, NHS, and More

Balancing therapies, sensory needs, school meetings, and daily life is stressful enough; adding financial worries makes it even more challenging. Many families are unaware of available funding sources, which can make a significant difference. Common options include Medicaid waivers, state disability programs, private insurance, and local grants. Medicaid often covers therapies, equipment, and respite care for eligible kids, regardless of income, in some states. State programs may provide monthly payments or access to special services. Private insurance can help, though you might need to appeal coverage denials. Local nonprofits, civic groups, and religious organizations sometimes offer grants for items like weighted blankets or AAC devices. Your county health department or social services office is a good starting point; they often have staff dedicated to disability resources who can guide you to more regional assistance.

In the UK, the NHS may fund therapy services or equipment through community pediatrics or speech and language therapy departments. You may also access help via your local council's Children with Disabilities team, especially if you are assessed as needing social care support.

Before applying, gather all necessary documents in one place. Most programs require a letter confirming your child's diagnosis from a doctor or psychologist (not just a school report), plus the latest IEP or 504 plan if available. Proof of income (recent pay stubs or tax returns) is usually required. Some grants also want quotes or invoices for services or equipment. Keeping a folder, paper or digital, of these documents saves time. A basic checklist:

- Medical diagnosis letter (from a licensed professional)
- IEP or 504 plan (if applicable)
- Recent proof of income
- Quotes for services/devices
- Insurance cards/information
- Proof of residence (utility bill, lease)

With these ready, you can apply quickly and efficiently respond to follow-up requests.

Applications usually request a short, personal statement about your child's needs. Stay factual but personal, explain how a device or therapy will change things. For example:

"A communication device will help Roman ask for help instead of crying."

"Respite care would give me a break so I can be more present for my child."

Attaching a photo of your child using a needed support can humanize your request.

Government forms can be confusing. If you're stuck, call the agency directly. Staff often expect questions and will be happy to walk you through the process. You can use a simple email to start:

"Hello, I'm looking for funding for my child's speech device. Could you tell me what programs might help and what documentation is required?"

Keep communications brief and clear; follow up in a week if you don't get a reply.

Respite care is an often-overlooked resource. County agencies or Medicaid waivers may cover the cost of trained caregivers, allowing you to rest or attend to errands. When inquiring:

"Hi, I'm interested in respite services for my son with autism. Can you send eligibility information and how to apply?"

In the UK, local councils may offer respite care (often called short breaks) as part of social care services. This support can be arranged through direct payment or commissioned services following an assessment. The NHS may also fund respite in certain complex cases through Continuing Care.

There may be waiting lists, so apply as soon as possible.

Connecting with local and online organizations is incredibly valuable. Autism-specific parent groups (in-person or on Facebook/WhatsApp) offer tips on funding, therapists, and which grants are processed quickly. Parents share sample letters, agency responsiveness, and encouragement. Inclusive sports leagues and sensory-friendly events provide a sense of community and understanding, allowing your child to be themselves and offering support from others who share a similar understanding.

Recreation programs often provide scholarships or sliding-scale fees for things like swimming lessons, art classes, or adapted camps. Don't hesitate to ask:

"Do you have scholarships for special needs families?"

Many programs do, but don't advertise.

It may feel uncomfortable to ask for help, but these resources exist to support families like yours. If you face roadblocks, connect with advocacy groups, they often assist with applications, appeals, or have volunteers familiar with the process.

Here's a simple template for grant or nonprofit inquiries:

"Dear [Organization], I am the parent of a young child with autism and need help with [therapy/equipment/respite]. Could you share details about available grants or your application process? Thank you for any information or support."

Being direct is efficient and shows you're ready to proceed.

Check back with organizations regularly, funding cycles change, and new opportunities can arise suddenly. Keep your documents updated so you're ready to apply when something comes up.

If the process feels overwhelming, take it step by step, contact one organization this week, organize your paperwork next week. Every step opens another opportunity. When your child receives therapy or equipment through one of these resources, all the paperwork will be worth it. Finding a supportive community where your family belongs makes a world of difference.

Handling Pushback—Advocating When Family or School Doesn't "Get It"

Sometimes, the toughest challenges aren't bureaucracy but the people around you who question, misunderstand, or resist. You might hear, "Why does she need all those visuals?" or "He just needs to try harder to fit in." Family may insist your child will "grow out of it," or say you're "coddling" by allowing stimming or refusing loud events. Schools might shrug off requests for sensory breaks with, "We treat everyone the same." This can be frustrating, isolating, and even make you doubt your instincts.

Facing skepticism is draining, yet common. When you encounter resistance, respond with clarity and confidence, using scripts anchored in your child's needs. For instance: "We use visual supports because they help Jordan understand, not because he's 'babyish.'" Or, "Autism is a lifelong difference, not something to 'outgrow.'" Speak plainly and assertively, not apologetically; this establishes boundaries. If a teacher claims your child is simply "acting out," gently clarify: "When Sam covers his ears, it's because he's overwhelmed by noise. He's coping, not being disrespectful." Repeating these explanations over time helps shift others' views.

Building allies means finding common ground and keeping communication open, even during disagreements. If a relative dismisses your choices, briefly share a relevant positive outcome: "Since we started using a timer for transitions, mornings are calmer." Sometimes, inviting others to observe strategies in practice does more than words. Encourage teachers to visit a therapy session or attend a parent workshop, supports work in real time can change minds. If educators push back, ask for a joint meeting with your child's support team. Emphasize shared goals, your child's learning and well-being, and invite collaboration: "Let's work together to help Alex succeed."

If your efforts stall and your child's needs are still unmet, if accommodations are denied or ignored, escalate your advocacy. Document every conversation, meeting, and email. Keep a simple log: date, attendees, topics, outcomes, or promises. Even brief notes after tense calls can help. Written records provide accountability and reveal patterns. If informal advocacy fails, request meetings in writing and reference relevant laws or policies ("Under Section 504, my child is entitled to reasonable accommodations"). If the school repeatedly refuses services or fails to follow plans, bring in outside help. A knowledgeable advocate, special education consultant, or legal advisor can guide and support you.

Filing a formal complaint may seem daunting but is sometimes necessary. Each district has its process; typically, you send a letter with a description of the issue and documentation of unmet needs. Stick to facts, attach supporting documents, and keep your tone respectful but firm. Focus on your child's right to access education and support. Occasionally, when rights are at risk, media or outside agencies may get involved, rarely, but sometimes powerfully so, when all else fails.

Through it all, remember that calm persistence is more effective than anger. Staying grounded protects your energy and keeps the focus on your child. Seeking support from other parents who understand these battles; they often have practical tips and perspective for difficult conversations and resilience.

Advocacy Log Template

Date

Person/Team

Issue Action Taken

Outcome/Notes

Try completing this table after each significant meeting or call, it helps you stay organized and track important details.

Advocacy often involves repetition and steady resolve. Each time you stand up for your child's needs and rights, you model self-advocacy, even when progress feels slow or thankless.

Advocating for your child can be lonely, especially when family or schools push back. Nonetheless, every conversation helps shift perspectives. Over time, your consistent clarity shows what your child truly needs to thrive, not just get by. Next, we'll focus on building family resilience and self-care along the way.

Chapter 7: Family, Friends, and the Wider World—Strengthening Your Support Network

Supporting Siblings—Age-Appropriate Explanations and Activities

Imagine an evening at home: kids playing, toys everywhere, laughter interspersed with occasional shrieks. Suddenly, your autistic child focuses on lining up blocks, while their sibling seeks attention or retreats in frustration. These ordinary moments capture the sibling dynamic, raising a child with autism while balancing the needs of their siblings can feel like walking a tightrope, with every emotion intensified. You want each child to feel seen and valued, though it's rarely simple.

Explain autism to siblings with honesty and gentle clarity. For young children, keep it simple: "Your brother's brain works in its own special way. He learns and plays differently, and things like loud noises or changes can upset him." For older siblings, be more detailed: "Autism means your sister's brain is wired uniquely. She might not talk as much or play the same way, but she has her own ways of expressing herself." Emphasize that autism is a difference, not a flaw. Encourage all questions, even the tough ones: "Why does he scream when we leave the park?" "Why can't she talk to me?"—and respond with openness and without shame.

Let siblings express any feelings they have. At times, they'll be proud or protective; other times, they may feel confused, jealous, or angry, especially when attention seems to revolve around meltdowns or therapy. Acknowledge these feelings as valid: say, "It can be hard when your sister needs extra help," or "It's okay if you're upset when things change suddenly." Don't promise things will always be fair but assure them you're there to listen and support.

Family activities can help everyone bond. Select routines where each child can participate at their own pace. Maybe it's a nightly dance party, have noise-canceling headphones ready for anyone who needs them, or a family walk with siblings alternating as leader. Parallel play often works well: set up art or building activities so everyone plays side-by-side, with occasional interaction but no pressure. Cooperative board or video games also promote teamwork, adapting rules as needed for all. Celebrate these moments with praise, photos, or a fun family cheer to reinforce the value of togetherness in all its forms.

Siblings may compete for attention or argue about what's "fair." To reduce rivalry, set aside one-on-one time with each child; even fifteen minutes of reading or chatting over hot chocolate helps, making sure this time is regular and protected. For younger children who feel left out during appointments, assign small "helper" roles like carrying toys, so they feel involved without feeling burdened. Older siblings may want more independence, such as extra screen time or time with friends, as a recognition of their flexibility.

Scripts can help in emotional moments. When jealousy surfaces, try: "I know you want more time with me alone. That matters; let's plan some time together this weekend." When frustration or confusion appears: "It seems like it's hard when your brother needs so much time. That's tough, I get it. Want to talk?" Giving language to big feelings helps siblings feel recognized instead of overlooked.

Include siblings in daily routines to build empathy and confidence. Let them help choose meals, plan outings, or pick a movie; these small decisions remind them they have a voice. Rotate "leader" roles for activities so that everyone has a turn being in charge, with support as needed. Celebrate siblings' strengths and interests just as much as therapy milestones, whether it's learning to ride a bike or winning a spelling bee.

Reflection Exercise: Sibling Connection Journal

Each week, jot down a moment when your children connected, no matter how small, or a time one helped another: sharing a snack, building together, or comforting each other. Invite siblings (when old enough) to add their own entries. Over time, these notes build a record of small victories and moments of joy, showing that connection grows through everyday experiences.

Supporting siblings means making space for every emotion and finding creative ways to bridge differences. By honoring both the challenges and successes, you help each child feel important and included no matter what the next day brings.

Building Inclusive Family Rituals—Everyone Belongs

Creating family rituals for every member can feel overwhelming, especially when autism shapes your routines. Still, shared traditions can anchor everyone with a sense of belonging, if you're willing to let them flex and shift to fit real life. These rituals don't have to be elaborate or perfect. They can be as simple as pizza night, a weekly movie in pajamas, or a chaotic birthday song sung off-key. The magic is in ensuring these moments reflect everyone's needs and preferences, not just old habits or outside ideals.

Start by considering what feels special to each person in your family. Maybe one child loves a lively holiday dinner, while another feels overwhelmed after a few minutes. Your autistic child might find comfort in a bedtime chant or prefer the same breakfast every Saturday. Shape your traditions around these individual needs, rather than seeing them as limitations. If dinner candles bother a child due to sensory sensitivity, consider using a lamp or battery-operated lights instead. For kids who struggle with noisy singing, consider alternatives like clapping, drumming, or humming. Adapting rituals helps everyone participate in their own way.

Participation will look different for each family member. Some dive right in, others prefer to watch, take breaks, or join in for small parts only. A child may decorate one cookie and leave, returning later for more. Flexibility communicates that everyone belongs, even if they engage differently. Sometimes, spontaneous activities, like a "train parade" sparked by a train-loving child, can become your new favorite ritual. Embrace these joyful quirks when you spot them.

Celebrate unique strengths and interests by incorporating them into traditions, such as dinosaur-themed birthday cakes, music-loving kids creating family playlists, or personalizing routines with silly songs or secret handshakes. These touches allow kids to see themselves reflected in the family's identity.

Traditions should never be stressful tests or burdens. If something causes meltdowns, anxiety, or resistance, like group photos, noisy parties, or costume days, stop and reassess what matters most. Sometimes a tweak helps, such as scheduling events earlier, limiting crowds, or providing a quiet space with noise-canceling headphones and fidget toys. Skipping an event for your child's comfort is not failure, it's respect.

Seek ideas from other families facing similar challenges. Many create inclusive holidays by hosting sensory-friendly events, previewing celebrations with picture schedules, or setting up side-by-side activities, so kids engage at their own pace. Share strategies in support groups or ask your children for suggestions; often, they have great ideas.

When introducing new routines, involve the whole family in planning. Let kids choose which traditions matter most, vote on new ones, or adjust old favorites. Even if an idea flops, the process can turn into its own positive memory.

Traditions change as children grow and needs shift. A ritual that worked last year may be too much this year, and that's okay. Allow yourselves to let go of traditions that no longer serve you and create new ones that fit your family's needs now. Family identity is about creating shared meaning, not sticking rigidly to the past.

If tension builds around a tradition, frequent tears before visiting relatives or anxiety over performances, pause and check in with everyone. Acknowledge their feelings: "This seems tough right now. Should we do it differently this year?" Permit yourselves to opt out without guilt, knowing that being together means more than any single plan can achieve.

Celebrating each person's quirks and contributions deepens the connection beyond any formal ritual. Notice what makes your family laugh, what comforts you on hard days, and where genuine joy appears. These small acts and shared moments become the foundation of belonging, telling every member: you fit here, exactly as you are.

Explaining Autism to Extended Family and Friends—Scripts and Story Cards

Explaining autism to relatives and friends can feel like stepping into uncharted territory. You might worry about saying the wrong thing or facing blank stares. Many parents describe sitting across from a grandparent or longtime friend, heart pounding, as they search for the words that will help others understand. What you want most is for your child to be accepted, not pitied or misunderstood. It helps to remember that most people want to support you, they need a little help seeing what life looks like through your child's lens.

Start with language that fits your comfort level and your audience's knowledge. For relatives who might have limited exposure to autism, keep things straightforward and positive: "Autism means that Ethan's brain works in a unique way. He might communicate or play differently, and sometimes he gets overwhelmed by noise or changes in routine." For those who know a little more, you can add: "Autism isn't something bad or broken; it just means some parts of life are harder, and some are amazing. You'll notice he loves trains and can recite all the stops, but parties and surprises make him anxious. The tone here matters—use words that affirm your child's strengths and make it clear this isn't something to be "fixed."

Sometimes, relatives need more than just spoken words. Visual "story cards" or short letters can bridge the gap, especially if you feel nervous or want to give family members something to refer back to. A story card might feature a photo of your child and a few simple sentences: "This is Ava. She uses her iPad to talk when she feels shy. She loves animals and gives the best hugs when she's comfortable." These cards can be shared at family gatherings or sent ahead before holidays or visits. Letters work too. A few paragraphs sent by email can help set expectations: "We're excited for the reunion! You might notice that Sam covers his ears when things get loud. It isn't rudeness. he hears sounds much more strongly than most people."

Not everyone will immediately understand or accept your explanations. Relatives sometimes offer advice that stings—"If you just disciplined him more..." or "She'll grow out of it." In those moments, it's essential to set clear boundaries without burning bridges. You might say, "I appreciate that you care, but we're following guidance from our therapists and doctors." Or, "We've learned that what works for other kids doesn't always help here. Thank you for respecting our choices." If someone resists accommodations, say, grumbling about bringing a sensory kit to dinner or using a visual schedule at Grandma's house, be firm but kind: "This helps our child feel safe so we can all enjoy time together." Sometimes you'll need to repeat yourself more than once. It's frustrating, but consistency helps.

Enlisting extended family as allies starts with small, concrete requests. Ask a grandparent to read a favorite book alongside your child or invite an aunt to join in a quiet activity rather than pushing for hugs. If a cousin notices your child walking away from the crowd, explain that breaks are part of how your child copes, not an attempt to be rude. Many family members want to help but don't know how; give them roles like "snack buddy," "quiet room helper," or "art partner." These jobs foster connection and show your child that others are on their side.

Share wins with your support circle. Tell Grandma when her patience helped your child try something new, or text your friend after a successful playdate, even if it lasted five minutes. These updates reinforce that support and flexibility make a real difference. When relatives see progress, however small, they also feel invested.

If you sense resistance is rooted in fear or old beliefs, offer gentle education over time. Share a favorite resource, storybook, or website when the moment feels right. Sometimes sharing a short video about autism or an online article makes things click in ways that words alone can't manage.

Above all, keep your family's needs at the center. You don't owe anyone a performance; your only job is to protect your child's well-being and comfort. If someone refuses to respect boundaries after repeated tries, it's okay to limit time together or skip certain events. It isn't easy. Sometimes it feels like you're standing alone, but you're setting an example for your child about self-advocacy and self-worth.

Building understanding in your wider circle takes patience, repetition, and a bit of creativity. Each time you explain, offer a visual aid, or assert a boundary, you're planting seeds for deeper acceptance, not just for your child but for all children who don't fit the mold. Your willingness to educate and advocate ripples outward, changing how others see and welcome difference.

Social Skills in Real Life—Playdates, Community Events, and Clubs

Arranging playdates or group activities for your autistic child can feel like assembling a puzzle with missing pieces. You want your child to connect with others, but maybe you worry about awkward silences, sudden tears, or the unpredictable twists that come with new places and unfamiliar faces. The good news is, social skills don't have to be learned in a single afternoon or in huge groups. They grow best in low-pressure, familiar settings where your child feels safe enough to try, pause, and try again. Start by choosing one or two children your child already knows, maybe from school or therapy, and invite them to your home or a place your child enjoys. Think about what your child loves: trains, dinosaurs, and water tables. Build the activity around these interests. Keep the first playdate short, forty-five minutes to an hour at most, and stick to a clear plan: "First snack time, then building blocks." Limit activities to just two options initially. Too many choices can overwhelm both kids.

Preparation helps set everyone up for success. Use a simple visual schedule, photos or drawings showing what will happen next, or walk your child through the plan verbally before the friend arrives. A script like, "After we build towers, it's time for snack, then we'll play outside," helps anchor expectations. Role-play common scenarios ahead of time. You can act out greetings, sharing toys, or asking for space using stuffed animals or action figures. Practice possible sticking points: "What if you need a break?" "How do you say 'no thank you' if you don't want to share?" Give your child specific phrases or cards they can use—"I need some alone time," "Let's do something else," or even just holding up a break card. These tools reduce pressure and help your child advocate for their needs in real time.

During the playdate, stay nearby but let the kids lead as much as they can. Step in gently if things go off the rail-redirect with humor, offer choices, or suggest a new activity if frustration bubbles up. If your child withdraws or becomes overstimulated, it's not a failure; it's information about what feels safe and what's too much. Create a quiet space nearby with pillows, books, or fidgets where your child can retreat and reset as needed. Let the other child know it's okay to take breaks, too. Everyone benefits from knowing that pauses are allowed.

When you're ready to branch out into community activities, library story times, art classes, and sports clubs, look for programs that welcome neurodiverse children. Many places now offer sensory-friendly sessions or staff who understand different communication styles. Before signing up, visit the space together and meet organizers so your child knows what to expect. Ask about their approach to meltdowns or difficult moments: do they have a chill-out corner? Are staff trained to support children with unique needs? Don't be afraid to advocate for small changes, a visual schedule on the wall, permission to bring headphones, or advance notice of routine changes.

If misunderstandings arise, maybe another parent asks why your child is spinning or not saying hello. Respond with a brief explanation: "He communicates differently and sometimes needs extra time to warm up." Give your child language for these moments as well: "I'm feeling shy," or "I like to watch before I join." Support self-advocacy by modeling acceptance and showing that it's okay to interact in ways that feel comfortable for your child.

Overstimulation is common in group settings; watch for signals like covering ears, hiding under tables, or zoning out. When you spot these cues, quietly offer to step outside or use a calming tool. Sometimes, just a few minutes away from the noise can make all the difference. If things unravel completely, meltdown brewing or already underway, leave without apology. Honor your child's limits and let them know you're proud of their efforts, no matter how long you stayed.

Some families find that the community starts small, with one neighbor, a cousin, or another parent from a therapy group, and grows from there. Over time, you'll learn which environments bring out your child's confidence and which ones are best avoided for now. Celebrate every attempt at connection, even fleeting eye contact or a shared laugh, and remember that social growth doesn't follow a set timeline.

Keep experimenting with clubs and teams until you find the right fit. Some autistic children thrive in robotics clubs or coding classes where the structure is clear and their interests are shared. Others prefer music groups or hiking clubs that allow for movement and sensory breaks. Ask organizers about flexibility: can your child come late or leave early? Is there space to sit out an activity without being singled out? These small accommodations can turn an intimidating event into a positive experience.

Above all, focus on progress over perfection. Social skills aren't about fitting in at any cost, they're about helping your child build real relationships in ways that honor who they are and what they need most.

Each step forward matters, even if it doesn't look exactly as you imagined at first.

Handling Stares and Judgment—Comebacks and Coping Strategies

Standing in the cereal aisle, you sense it before you even look up, someone's gaze lingering a beat too long as your child rocks, flaps, or begins to cry. Maybe you hear the whisper or catch the pointed sigh from an older shopper who doesn't get why your child "acts that way." Sometimes, it's the unsolicited advice from a stranger, or the parent at the playground who suggests a quick fix for a meltdown she's never had to handle. The sting is real. Whether it's outright comments or just disapproving glances, being watched and judged while supporting your autistic child in public can rattle even the calmest parent. These moments hit hard because they poke at your deepest wish: for your child to be accepted, not scrutinized.

In these situations, it's easy to freeze, feel ashamed, or want to disappear. But you deserve tools that let you stand tall. Sometimes a simple script is enough to set boundaries without inviting conflict. Try, "He's having a hard time—thanks for your patience," or "She's autistic, so things are different for her." If someone offers advice you didn't ask for, a polite but firm, "We're working closely with his team—thank you," can close the door. When words feel impossible, even a calm nod or turning away can send a message: you're focused on your child's needs, not anyone else's approval. Save your energy for what matters.

For those days when stares feel relentless, remember that you don't owe anyone an explanation. If you sense judgment brewing and don't have the words or emotional bandwidth to engage, it's okay to leave carts behind, skip the checkout line, or walk out of noisy spaces. Your child's dignity and sense of safety matter more than any stranger's fleeting opinion. Shielding your child from harsh eyes, by crouching to their level, using a favorite blanket, or simply stepping between them and the crowd, isn't overprotective; it's compassionate parenting.

Stress in these moments can sneak up on you, tight shoulders, shallow breath, racing heart. Practicing self-regulation techniques can help you stay steady. Focus on your breath: inhale deeply through your nose, count to four, and exhale slowly through your mouth. Ground yourself by noticing five things around you, the sound of music overhead, the cool air from a freezer, the color of cereal boxes. This brings you back to the moment and out of the swirl of judgment. Sometimes, repeating a quiet mantra—"My child comes first," "We're okay," or even "This will pass"—can anchor you when emotions threaten to spill over.

Some parents find it helpful to rehearse comebacks ahead of time, so they feel less caught off guard. "He isn't misbehaving—he's communicating differently," or "We all have tough days; thanks for understanding," can be practiced at home until they roll off your tongue without effort. Others prefer using humor to defuse tension: "We're just adding some excitement to aisle four!" Not every situation calls for words; sometimes, just walking away is most powerful.

Community-driven support can make all the difference in reframing these experiences. Connect with other parents who have stood in your shoes. They'll share stories of public meltdowns and offer validation that you're not failing. Many families swap their favorite responses or make "resilience cards"—small business-sized notes explaining autism that they hand out if they're too tired to speak. Some parents wear discreet pins or bracelets that quietly signal "autism family" status, helping others recognize what's going on and sometimes inviting solidarity rather than side-eye.

It helps to remember that most people staring aren't truly cruel; often, they're curious, uninformed, or anxious themselves. When you have extra energy, use these moments as tiny teachable opportunities; a brief explanation today might mean fewer stares for another family tomorrow. But on days when advocacy feels impossible, give yourself permission to focus only on your child and your own well-being.

Resilience grows not from brushing off every hurt but from recognizing which battles are worth fighting and which are best left behind. Give yourself credit each time you navigate public spaces with your child's needs at the forefront. Over time, these experiences can shift from being about shame to being about pride in your ability to protect and prioritize what truly matters: your child's emotional safety and sense of belonging. Every time you choose compassion for your child over comfort for bystanders, you show both yourself and your child what real strength looks like.

Finding Your Village—Support Groups, Online Communities, and Peer Mentors

There's a particular loneliness that can settle in after an autism diagnosis, even when you're surrounded by people. You might feel like nobody truly gets the daily ups and downs, except for the other parents sitting in therapy waiting rooms or swapping exhausted glances at the playground. Finding your village isn't just about gathering advice; it's about being seen, understood, and accepted by those who know what it's like to celebrate a new word or endure a public meltdown. The first step is simply realizing you don't have to figure it all out on your own.

Start by looking for local support groups through schools, clinics, or community centers. Many cities and towns host regular meetups, coffee mornings, or playgroups where parents of children with autism gather, sometimes alongside professionals, and sometimes just as peers. These spaces offer a safe place to share stories or vent frustrations without fear of judgment. In-person groups allow for the beauty of real-time connection, a shared smile, a knowing nod, the comfort of physical presence. There's something grounding about sitting in a room with others who understand your shorthand, your acronyms, your daily challenges. You may walk in as strangers, but leave feeling lighter simply because someone else said, "Us too."

Of course, not everyone can access in-person groups easily. That's where online communities come alive. Forums, Facebook groups, Reddit threads, and nonprofit message boards connect families across time zones and continents. These digital spaces allow you to reach out at midnight when you can't sleep or read stories from parents whose children are older (or younger) than yours. You'll find practical tips. how to set up a visual schedule, which sensory toys really work, but also solidarity on hard days. Online groups can be a lifeline for rural families or those juggling impossible schedules, and anonymity gives some people freedom to speak honestly about struggles they'd never share face-to-face.

Still, online support isn't without pitfalls. Misinformation can spread quickly, and not every group is affirming or well-moderated. Sometimes posts spiral into negativity or "parent shaming." It's wise to lurk for a while before joining discussions, notice whether members support each other, and whether group rules encourage respect and inclusion. Avoid any space that pushes miracle cures or undermines your instincts as a parent. You deserve compassion and real help, not guilt trips or toxic advice.

Peer mentorship adds another layer of support that's uniquely powerful. Connecting with a parent who's further along this path, or even an autistic adult who can share their lived experience, can change everything. Mentors offer practical wisdom that no textbook can provide; they've navigated IEP meetings, survived public meltdowns, and figured out what works (or doesn't) for their own families. Some organizations pair new parents with seasoned mentors for regular check-ins, phone calls, or texts. Others host Q&A panels where you can ask anything—from school tips to self-care hacks, and hear honest answers.

Don't underestimate the value of connecting with autistic adults who are willing to share their perspectives. Their voices can challenge assumptions, broaden your understanding of what's possible, and remind you that your child's future holds hope and joy alongside its challenges. If you're unsure where to start, look for advocacy organizations or social media accounts run by autistic people themselves. These are often great sources of firsthand insight.

The most important thing is to keep showing up, even if it's just reading along quietly at first. Over time, you'll gather not only resources but relationships that help sustain you through setbacks and celebrate small victories. Community participation doesn't mean turning every problem into a group project; sometimes it's just about being reminded that there are others out there rooting for your child and for you.

You might be surprised by how much knowledge is tucked away in these networks: recommendations for therapists who truly listen, advice on navigating school meetings without losing your cool, creative solutions for daily routines that don't show up in parenting books. These shared experiences are gold.

Keep yourself open to new information and perspectives. Take what fits your family and leave the rest behind. As you gain confidence, pay it forward, share your own successes and stumbles so that families just starting out know they aren't alone either.

Support networks shift with time; friends come and go, needs change as children grow older or challenges evolve. That's normal. What matters is knowing you always have somewhere to turn, a village ready to listen, lift you up, and remind you that progress is possible even on the roughest days.

As we wrap up this chapter about building connections with family, friends, and community, remember that no one raises a child in isolation. The right support turns confusion into clarity and loneliness into belonging. Up next: nurturing your own wellbeing and keeping hope alive for the long run, because thriving as a family starts with caring for yourself too.

Chapter 8:
Hope, Growth, and Self-Care—Sustaining Your Journey Together

Preventing Burnout—Five-Minute Self-Care Routines for Busy Parents

Parenting often means the house finally falls quiet at night, yet your mind races and true rest remains elusive. Many parents end up scrolling on their phones late, searching for a brief "me time," even if it means less sleep. This constant state of vigilance isn't just ordinary tiredness; it leads to burnout, that deeper sense of running on empty. Yet, you continue to give, even when you feel depleted.

Here's what matters: micro self-care is essential, not optional. These small moments aren't rewards; they're vital for survival. Your well-being is the foundation for your child's growth. If you're running on fumes, both your patience and creativity diminish. Fortunately, you don't need long breaks or special trips to recharge. Effective self-care can be incorporated into your daily routine in quick, five-minute increments. Instead of grand overhauls, focus on tiny habits, little resets that keep you afloat amid the hectic flow of family life. Remember: sustainable care for your child is built on sustainable self-care for you. Research from Arizona Autism United supports the idea that even brief self-care routines directly bolster your resilience and help you be the parent you aspire to be (see Source 1 in APA list).

The key is finding five-minute "windows" throughout your day, small anchors that offer clarity, relief, and renewed patience. While waiting in the school line, use the opportunity for deep breathing: inhale through your nose for four counts, hold briefly, and then exhale through your mouth. Cycle this a few times, noticing tension release from your body.

Or, cue up a three-minute guided meditation or body scan on your phone to help release stress.

Turn everyday tasks into mindful moments. While making coffee or tea after school drop-off, pause to actually notice the warmth, steam, and aroma; let worries fade and simply be present for a few minutes. Gentle, quick stretches, reach up, roll your shoulders, or shake out your limbs, can help restore energy and relieve stiffness. Fit these in while your child is entertained for a moment or during brief lulls in routine.

If even brief self-care feels impossible, or if guilt tries to keep you from it, give yourself a "permission slip." Place a sticky note somewhere visible: "Caring for myself helps me care for my child." Remind yourself, "My needs matter too." These affirmations aren't self-indulgent; they're essential.

It's common for parents to feel there's no time or space for themselves, but self-care can be embedded into family life. Try instituting a five-minute "family quiet time" after lunch or before bed. Everyone, adults and children, can read, listen to music, doodle, or simply lie quietly. With this modeled consistently, even young children will adapt, and the whole family benefits from a pause.

If you need more practical, real-life ideas, here's a quick go-to menu:

- Deep breathing while waiting in the car or in line.
- Mindful coffee/tea moments in the kitchen.
- Five-minute guided meditations via free apps.
- Gentle stretching during the kids' TV time.
- Listening to a favorite song with headphones.
- Stepping outside for fresh air and a few deep breaths.

Interactive Element: Five-Minute Self-Care Menu

Keep this list handy, tape it inside a cabinet or save it on your phone. Each is short enough not to be disrupted by life's interruptions.

If time or guilt feel like barriers, pair self-care with basic tasks: play music while cooking or stretch while supervising bath time. Remember, consistent small actions lead to lasting change.

When you demonstrate self-care, you teach your child that everyone's needs matter. It models resilience and healthy ways to manage stress. Family quiet time isn't just a break; it sets boundaries and helps everyone recharge.

You're not expected to run on empty to prove yourself as a loving or effective parent. Small, regular self-care steps are non-negotiable for raising an autistic child with strength and hope. Strong roots let you weather the tough days and enjoy the bright moments ahead (see Source 1 in APA list).

Managing Guilt and Comparison—Reframing Progress and Success

It's common to find yourself late at night, scrolling through social media, comparing your daily chaos with the seemingly perfect family moments posted by others: kids smiling, milestones reached, awards won. Meanwhile, your own day may have ended with a meltdown in the cereal aisle and an untouched dinner. A feeling of inadequacy or guilt often follows as you wonder, "Why can't I do more?" This "comparison trap" can be relentless and sneaky.

Guilt and self-doubt are nearly universal among parents, especially those raising autistic children. You want the best for your child, so you search for reassurance by measuring yourself against what you see around you. But social media snapshots and playground stories rarely show the reality behind the scenes. Everyone's journey is more complex than it appears.

Some parents have shared how painful it feels to compare their child's progress with others. For example, a mom once described seeing another child talk in full sentences while her own son still used gestures, and a dad admitted feeling shame when his daughter couldn't handle a noisy family gathering. These moments sting because we tend to measure our lives against others, but snapshots don't show the daily effort and love you pour into moving forward.

Think of progress as a winding forest path rather than a straight, sunny road. Some days, you may stumble or need to backtrack. Your child's path might twist away from expectations, but it's beautiful and meaningful, shaped by their unique needs and strengths rather than anyone else's timeframe. When comparison creeps in and you think, "We're falling behind," pause and ask: "Is this really true, or am I using someone else's standard?" Your family's progress is unique, based on your personal mix of strengths and challenges.

Reframing takes time and practice. A helpful tool is to extend the same kindness to yourself that you offer others. When negative self-talk appears, like "I failed" or "I'm not enough," imagine what you'd say if a friend voiced these worries: "You're doing your best. Progress is different for everyone." Try saying or writing these supportive responses, as hearing them in your own words can make a difference.

Simple reminders can help reinforce this mindset. Sticky notes with affirmations, such as "Progress is progress" or "Small steps are real steps," posted on your mirror or fridge, can help anchor your thinking. If you like visuals, sketch a winding path and add a mark for each small win or shift in perspective.

Curate your environment for your well-being. If certain social media accounts make you feel inadequate, it's okay to mute or unfollow them. Instead, engage in spaces that offer genuine support, like starting a text thread with one or two understanding friends where you can share honest struggles and small victories. Real connection, sometimes just a "Me too"—can ease shame and restore perspective.

If you notice yourself spiraling into guilt or comparison, ground yourself in the present. Ask, "What went well today, even if it was tiny?" Perhaps your child made eye contact, played quietly for a few minutes, or managed to get through the school drop-off without shedding a tear. These moments deserve celebration just as much as bigger milestones.

Remember, the loudest voices of criticism in your mind aren't always the truest. Even the most put-together parents have difficult days and worries about the future. Your efforts matter, regardless of how different your journey may appear. Allow your family to move at its own pace and celebrate what's real for you, not what looks perfect for someone else.

If you need a reminder, ask: "Would I speak this way to my best friend?" If not, extend yourself the patience and encouragement you'd offer them. Replace criticism with compassion. Your progress is real, even if it doubles back sometimes. Your love is clear in every choice you make for your child, that's more than enough.

Celebrating Bright Spots—Milestone Logs and Strengths-Based Journaling

In the busyness of daily routines and appointments, it's easy to miss moments of progress, especially the small, meaningful ones. You may find yourself fixating on what went wrong: a meltdown, an argument, dinner on the floor. These moments stick, but so can bright spots, if you intentionally notice and record them. That's where a milestone log or "bright spot" journal can help. This isn't just for major achievements; it's about collecting small victories, a new word whispered at bedtime, a spontaneous hug, a peaceful morning routine. These bits of progress are easy to forget unless you write them down.

A milestone log doesn't have to be elaborate. Use a notebook, a phone app, or even a piece of paper on the fridge. At week's end, jot down what stood out, trying a new food, waving at a neighbor, five minutes of independent play. Prompts can help: "Today my child…" followed by something meaningful, made eye contact, put on socks, looked at a book, asked for help without tears. Over time, this creates a record of growth much richer than any report card or assessment.

Moving from deficit-based tracking to a strengths-based outlook takes effort. Standard systems tend to highlight what your child can't do, focusing on delays and unmet therapy goals. But your child isn't just a checklist; they're a mix of abilities, quirks, and small successes. Capturing the good, even very minor highlights, helps you see patterns of resilience and capability. Maybe your child lined up toys by color for the first time, wore a new shirt without protest, or smiled at their siblings. These count as much as bigger milestones.

Make celebration part of everyday life, not something saved for rare occasions. Get creative: set up a "success wall" with sticky notes, index cards, or photos to display achievements where everyone can see. Each family member can add their own: "Sam tried broccoli," "Mom handled a tough phone call," "We survived Monday." Such reminders build community and show that everyone's efforts are noticed and important.

Some families have monthly celebration nights, after dinner, each person shares something that went well, no matter how small: "I remembered my backpack," or "We finished a puzzle together." Light candles, have dessert, or play a favorite song - whatever brings joy to your family. This ritual marks progress and encourages connection, even during challenging times.

Progress isn't always steady. Sometimes there are setbacks or slow weeks. In those times, recognize the hard things you managed anyway, such as getting out the door after a meltdown or remaining calm when your child refused dinner repeatedly. These moments show grit and unwavering love. Use your journal to reflect on how you coped, even if things weren't picture perfect. Revisiting these entries later reminds you how much has changed, especially when progress feels invisible.

If you're not into writing, try voice memos or photos, snap your child's block tower, record a favorite song, or video a new dance. Flip through these when you need encouragement. Progress isn't always headline-worthy; sometimes it's a quiet smile after tears or a brave try after a setback.

To get started, here's a basic weekly template:

Weekly Milestone Log Template

- New word(s) attempted:
- Social attempt (wave, smile, greeting):
- Act of independence (self-dressing, helping with chores):
- Favorite moment:
- Challenge handled (how you coped):
- Something we celebrated:

Keep this template where you'll see it, a kitchen drawer, bedside table, or on your phone, to make it a habit.

Celebrating bright spots isn't about ignoring hardship but about deliberately noticing hope in everyday life and teaching your child that growth is about effort as well as outcome. These small acts of noticing and acknowledging fuel you for another day and help your family see just how much is possible.

Planning for the Future—Transition Skills and Future Files

Thinking ahead about your child's future can feel daunting, but planning starts with breaking big goals into small, manageable steps tailored to your child's personality, interests, and needs. Independence isn't achieved all at once; it develops through simple skills, habits, and choices over time. Start early, young children can practice transition skills by helping pick groceries or pressing a checkout button. These everyday moments teach confidence and life skills.

Life skills are the foundation of independence and can be integrated into daily routines from a young age. Encourage your child to check items off a visual calendar to learn about time and planning. A small allowance, coins or tokens, can teach basic money concepts like saving, counting, and making choices at the store. Every small decision, such as choosing a snack, builds real-world decision-making abilities and prepares your child for bigger choices later on.

Self-advocacy can also begin early, regardless of your child's communication style. Even limited verbal skills allow for practicing asking for help using gestures, pictures, or devices. Try simple role-plays, like how to ask for assistance, say "stop," or request a break. Model this behavior yourself to show that asking for help is normal and wise. As your child learns to express needs, they gain the confidence to speak up in various settings.

Organizing for the future is key, and a "Future File" can help. This living document gathers all essential information in one place and grows with your child. Start by organizing school records, IEPs, report cards, teacher notes, since these are often needed for new schools or services. Add medical information: diagnosis letters, allergy lists, therapy and medication records. As your child gets older, include legal documents like guardianship papers or benefits details. The system doesn't need to be perfect; the important thing is knowing where things are when you need them.

As adolescence approaches, planning adapts to new changes. Puberty brings physical and emotional shifts, so establish clear routines for hygiene and self-care. Use visual, step-by-step instructions for showering, using deodorant, and dental care. Start these lessons early to prevent confusion or overwhelm. Use concrete language and visuals to discuss bodies, privacy, and boundaries, crucial topics for autistic children who benefit from clarity.

Talk openly about relationships and sexuality before formal education covers these areas. Discuss safe touch, consent, and personal boundaries early. Weave these conversations into everyday life to make them less uncomfortable. Begin with body parts and privacy in early childhood; introduce puberty basics around ages ten or eleven; and expand on relationships and safety as your child matures.

Including your child in transition planning is empowering. Bring them into IEP meetings, even if just briefly, or let them choose a personal goal (like making breakfast or taking the bus). If full meetings are overwhelming, let your child decide when to participate, or give them choices beforehand. For broader decisions, ask what activities or future jobs interest them.

Building a support team is as vital as teaching skills. Mentors might be a supportive teacher, an older relative, or an after-school leader. Trusted adults outside the family offer encouragement that can be especially meaningful. As your child matures, having a network of supportive adults makes new transitions smoother.

Staying organized helps avoid feeling overwhelmed. Checklists for transition planning are useful, such as:

- Practice using a weekly planner.
- Teach money basics with allowance and counting coins.
- Develop step-by-step hygiene cards.
- Schedule regular "future talks" about school or home goals.
- Update the "Future File" annually with new documents.
- Identify a new mentor or trusted adult each term.
- Begin puberty discussions by age ten.
- Practice asking for help in various settings.
- Review legal documents as needed (especially before age 18).

Independence isn't rushed or linear, but steady practice and planning enable your child to become their own advocate. Each new skill adds to their ability to make choices and take more control over their future.

Promoting Self-Advocacy—Empowering Your Child's Voice

Self-advocacy is the practice of knowing and speaking up for your own needs, preferences, and boundaries. For autistic children, this skill isn't just helpful, it's life-changing. The phrase "Nothing about me without me" says it all: your child deserves to be part of every conversation and decision that affects them, from daily routines to school supports. When kids learn early that their voice matters, they grow up more confident and able to shape their world in ways that fit them. Even very young children can start learning these skills, and it's never too early or too late to begin.

Empowering self-advocacy starts with recognizing and naming needs. Encourage your child to notice when they're hungry, tired, overwhelmed, or need a break. Use everyday choices, picking between two snacks, choosing which shirt to wear, or deciding on a bedtime story, as natural practice. These small decisions build the foundation for bigger acts of self-direction later. You can also create simple opportunities for your child to say "no" safely. For example, during play, ask, "Do you want a hug, or would you rather high-five?" If they refuse, respect it fully. This teaches that "no" is respected and safe to use.

Daily routines are full of chances to practice self-advocacy. Role-play scenarios like asking for a break at school or using a break card when things get too noisy. Show your child how to use words, gestures, or pictures to communicate their needs. For non-speaking kids or those who use AAC, visual support can be powerful tools. Create "My Needs" cards for home and school settings, simple visuals or written phrases such as "I need quiet," "Help please," or "All done." Practice using these cards together so they become familiar and easy to grab in real situations.

Scripts can help make new skills less intimidating. Start with sentence starters like "I feel…" and "I need…" and model their use: "I feel tired, I need five minutes alone." Repeat this in your own life so your child sees self-advocacy in action. When you call the school to request an accommodation or tell a friend you can't make it because you're exhausted, narrate the process out loud: "I'm letting Mrs. Smith know we need a quieter space for the meeting because loud rooms are hard for me." This normalizes asking for what you need and shows your child that even grown-ups self-advocate.

Building self-advocacy takes patience, repetition, and encouragement. Celebrate every attempt, whether your child points to a picture, types a word on their device, or simply shakes their head when something doesn't work for them. Each effort is both a form of communication and a demonstration of self-determination. Some families create a mini poster with common scripts by the front door so kids can practice before leaving for school, such as: "Can I have more time?" "I need help." "No thank you." Over time, these scripts become second nature.

Real-life stories demonstrate the power of self-advocacy at any age. Take Maya, a seven-year-old who uses AAC at school. At first, she struggled to tell her teacher when she was overwhelmed by noise. After months with her "I need quiet" card taped to her desk, she began holding it up herself when things got too much. Her teacher learned to respond by offering headphones or a short walk outside. Maya's mother noticed fewer meltdowns and more smiles at pick-up time, proof that even simple tools can open up possibilities.

Another example comes from Jack, a twelve-year-old who'd always hated gym class because of the echo in the gymnasium. His parents worked with him on a script: "The echo hurts my ears. Can I use headphones?" With practice at home, Jack felt brave enough to say this to his teacher. The school allowed him to wear headphones during gym, which made him more willing to participate and less likely to shut down.

The most effective self-advocacy is collaborative, not just about demanding needs but about helping others understand and meet them together. In therapy sessions, encourage your child to express preferences: "Do you want to start with puzzles or blocks?" Therapists can reinforce this by honoring choices and asking for feedback throughout the session. When kids see adults listening and adjusting based on their input, they learn that speaking up leads to positive change.

Self-advocacy isn't only for older children or those who use speech fluently. Even young children or those who are non-verbal can learn to express their needs through visuals, gestures, or technology. The key is consistency: ensuring that every adult in your child's life —teachers, therapists, family —respects and responds to their voice in whatever form it takes.

Over time, these skills grow with your child. The payoff is enormous: more independence, fewer behavioral struggles rooted in frustration, and a deep sense of being respected for who they are. You'll see your child not just following routines but actively shaping their world so it fits them better, one choice, one request at a time.

Staying Current—Building Your Personalized Resource Toolkit

The world of autism support, therapies, and advocacy is constantly in motion. New research emerges frequently, opinions shift, and what worked last year may require a fresh perspective. As a parent, it's easy to feel like you're playing catch-up. When daily routines already swamp you, how do you keep up with all the changes? The secret is to build a living, breathing toolkit—one that keeps you connected to the best information, support, and community, without overwhelming you.

Start by handpicking sources you trust. Not every website or social media page deserves your time. Focus on established organizations like the National Autistic Society, Autism Speaks, and your country's major autism associations. These are usually reliable for understanding rights, therapies, and new findings. Podcasts such as the "Autism Science Foundation Podcast" or "The Autism Dad" offer research updates in a friendly, digestible format. For more clinical perspectives, look for resources from reputable medical centers or universities. Email newsletters from neurodiversity-affirming organizations are goldmines for the latest research and tips; they come straight to your inbox, saving you from endless searching.

But not every shiny new article or app is worth your trust. Before you add something to your toolkit, check who wrote it. Is the author a credentialed professional or a self-proclaimed expert? Does the resource cite recent studies, or is it mostly opinion? Look for evidence backing up claims, peer-reviewed journals, references to controlled studies, or clear links to established guidelines. If a therapy sounds too good to be true or pushes miracle cures, that's a red flag. Trust your instincts and seek consensus from multiple sources. If you're ever in doubt, bring the information to your child's speech therapist or pediatrician for their input.

The organization transforms chaos into confidence. Digital tools make this easier than ever. I recommend setting up a Google Drive folder labeled "Autism Toolkit." Inside, create subfolders: "Therapies," "School Supports," "Legal/Financial," "Communication Tools," and "Favorite Articles." Save PDFs, links, and scanned notes from meetings so everything is easy to find when you need it, no more panicked searches through email at 10 p.m. For those who prefer paper, a simple binder with color-coded tabs can be a great solution. Some parents use note apps like Evernote or Apple Notes, tagging each entry by topic for quick access.

Technology can also automate your learning process. Setting up Google alerts for terms like "autism research" or "speech therapy autism" brings fresh studies and news straight to you, no more hunting required. Follow select accounts on social media that consistently share evidence-based updates; mute the rest if they don't bring value. Sign up for newsletters from groups that align with your values; these often include event invites, webinars, and advocacy updates.

Don't forget the power of community. Sharing resources multiplies their value. Host a resource swap with friends or fellow parents, either in person with printouts and favorite books or online, where you exchange links and app recommendations. These gatherings are less about perfection and more about learning from each other's lived experiences. In support groups or parent forums, offer your best finds, a checklist you made for school meetings, an app that finally helped with visual schedules, and ask others what's made a difference for them. What works in one family might spark an idea or solution for yours.

As your child grows and their needs change, so will your toolkit. Review it every few months, archive what's outdated, and highlight new gems. Encourage older children to participate in this process as well; let them choose a favorite communication app or help organize their own files. This not only lightens your mental load but also models lifelong learning and adaptability.

Visual Element: Sample Google Drive "Autism Toolkit" Structure

- Main Folder: Autism Toolkit
    - Therapies (speech, OT, play therapy PDFs)
    - School Supports (IEP templates, teacher letters)
    - Communication Tools (visual schedules, AAC guides)
    - Legal/Financial (funding forms, benefits info)
    - Favorite Articles & Podcasts

Print this structure or set it up digitally for instant clarity.

Staying current doesn't mean knowing everything; it means having a system to find, filter, and share what matters most as new questions arise. Filling your toolkit with solid resources lets you adapt confidently to whatever comes next. And when you share what you've learned, you help strengthen the whole community of parents and caregivers around you.

In this chapter, we've explored ways to sustain hope and growth through thoughtful self-care, celebration of progress, planning for tomorrow, empowering your child's voice, and building a resource toolkit that evolves alongside your family's needs. By staying organized and connected to quality information and community support, you make space for both stability and flexibility, laying the groundwork for whatever comes next in your child's unique story.

A Humble Request!

Your voice matters, because another parent might be where you once were.

If this guide helped you breathe easier on hard days, brought new hope to your child's progress, or simply reminded you that you're not alone, you have a story worth sharing.

As a fellow parent or caregiver navigating the ups and downs of autism, your feedback could be the turning point for someone searching for answers at 2 a.m., feeling overwhelmed and unsure where to begin.

💬 *Did a strategy in the book reduce your child's meltdowns? Help with transitions? Spark a breakthrough in communication?*

Please take a moment to leave an honest review on Amazon. It doesn't need to be long, just real. Your words could make all the difference for another family.

♡ **Thank you for being part of this supportive community. Together, we're making the journey a little easier, one step at a time.**

For eBook readers – click on the link below.

For print book, scan the QR code.

Conclusion

If you've made it to this final chapter, maybe with a coffee gone cold by your side, or after reading in short bursts between appointments and bedtime routines, I want to pause and say: Thank you. Thank you for showing up, again and again, for your child and your family. Thank you for trusting me to walk with you through some of the messiest, hardest, and most beautiful corners of autism parenting. I'm writing this not just as a therapist, but as someone who has sat with thousands of families, listened to fears and hopes, and witnessed countless small miracles in daily life. My goal with this book has always been to offer you something real: practical, evidence-based tools, a judgment-free place to land, and a strong dose of hope.

We began this journey by acknowledging what many parents feel but rarely say out loud: this path can be overwhelming. The moment you first suspected autism, the flood of questions, the nights spent wondering what the future holds—these are universal. But so is your child's spark. Together, we unpacked what autism really means, moving beyond outdated labels and myths, and into the vibrant reality of neurodiversity. We looked closely at early signs, unique strengths, and the power of seeing your child's profile as more than a diagnosis—a living, breathing "owner's manual" that changes and grows with them.

We dug into connection, the bedrock of all progress. We discussed tuning in to your child's cues, meeting them where they are, and allowing play and shared joy to build trust. We explored communication in all its forms, spoken words, gestures, AAC, scripts, and everything in between. Whether your child "talks" with their hands, their device, or their eyes, you learned ways to honor and expand their voice. We tackled meltdowns and sensory storms, not with shame or punishment, but with real-world co-regulation, calming toolkits, and the power of routines that flex for your unique family.

You built structure, morning routines, bedtime rituals, and transition plans that make daily life less chaotic. You learned to use visuals, choice boards, and micro-routines to smooth out bumps and celebrate every small victory. We examined advocacy: how to navigate school meetings, communicate with teachers, and sift through therapy options with a critical yet hopeful eye. We didn't shy away from controversy, like the debate around ABA. Instead, I encouraged you to trust your instincts, ask tough questions, and prioritize your child's voice above all.

We also moved outward, into family, friendships, and community. You found ways to support siblings, adapt traditions, and handle stares and judgment in public. You learned that it's okay to set boundaries with relatives or let go of old routines that no longer serve your family. Community matters. Whether it's an online group, a neighbor who "gets it," or a peer mentor, you are never meant to do this alone.

At every step, I tried to show you that *progress is possible*—and that it doesn't have to look like anyone else's. Every autistic child is unique. There is no script, no universal milestone chart. Connection always comes before correction. Strengths-based approaches are not just buzzwords; they are the path to confidence and real growth. The strategies and exercises we've shared can be reshaped and tweaked to suit your child, your routines, your energy level, and even your challenging days. If you remember nothing else, remember this: you are your child's most powerful advocate, and your relationship with them is what matters most.

I know this journey is not always easy. There will be days when you feel exhausted, unseen, or judged. There will be times you doubt your decisions or worry that you're not doing enough. Please hear me: these feelings are normal. Parenting a neurodivergent child asks so much of you. But you are also resilient. Your child's progress, however winding, is a testament to your love and persistence. Celebrate the bright spots, every smile, every new word, every meltdown weathered and repaired. These are victories, no matter how small.

Keep learning. The world of autism is always changing, as are your child's needs. Build your own resource toolkit. Stay curious. Connect with other parents, listen to autistic adults, and seek out new ideas as your child grows. Adapt. What works today might need tweaking tomorrow, and that's okay.

Above all, please take care of yourself. Your well-being is not a luxury; it's a foundation. Five minutes for a cup of tea, a walk outside, or a favorite song can reset your day—model self-care for your children. Let them see that everyone's needs, including yours, are important. Lean on your village, family, friends, support groups, and professionals for support. Let others step in, even when it feels hard to ask.

If there's one message I hope stays with you, it's this: Progress is worth celebrating, perfection is not required. Setbacks will happen. Some days will be messy and loud. Others will be soft and full of laughter. Notice the bright spots. Write them down, share them with your partner or a trusted friend, and look back on them in the more challenging moments. Growth is rarely linear, but every step forward, no matter how small, builds confidence and hope.

So here's my invitation, from one advocate to another: Trust your instincts. Use the scripts, routines, and tools that fit your family, and don't be afraid to let go of what doesn't. Speak up in meetings. Share your child's strengths. Adapt, adjust, and redefine success as often as you need. You know your child better than anyone. You are the expert on your family. And you are absolutely the advocate your child needs.

Thank you for letting me be a part of your journey. I am deeply grateful for your dedication, courage, and willingness to continue learning and loving in the face of uncertainty. Remember, no matter how isolated you feel, you are not alone. There is a community of parents, professionals, and autistic voices cheering you on. Together, we can create lives for our children that are joyful, connected, and full of possibility. Your family's story matters. Keep going. I'm rooting for you, every step of the way.

References

- American Speech-Language-Hearing Association. (n.d.). Augmentative and alternative communication (AAC). Retrieved July 19, 2025, from https://www.asha.org/public/speech/disorders/aac/
- Autism Parenting Magazine. (n.d.). Assistive Communication Devices for Children with Autism. Retrieved July 19, 2025, from https://www.autismparentingmagazine.com/assistive-technology-autism/
- Autism Spectrum News. (n.d.). The neuro-strength-based support framework. Retrieved July 19, 2025, from https://autismspectrumnews.org/the-neuro-strength-based-support-framework-a-collaborative-strength-focused-approach-to-autism-interventions/
- Autism Treatment Center. (n.d.). The difference between meltdowns & tantrums. Retrieved July 19, 2025, from https://autismtreatmentcenter.org/knowledge-base/the-difference-between-meltdowns-and-tantrums/
- Autism UK. (n.d.). Autism and neurodiversity. Retrieved July 19, 2025, from https://www.autism.org.uk/advice-and-guidance/topics/identity/autism-and-neurodiversity
- Autism UK. (n.d.). What happens during an autism assessment. Retrieved July 19, 2025, from https://www.autism.org.uk/advice-and-guidance/topics/diagnosis/assessment-and-diagnosis/what-happens-during-an-autism-assessment

- Autism Classroom Resources. (n.d.). Visual schedule series: First-Then schedules (Freebie!). Retrieved July 19, 2025, from https://autismclassroomresources.com/visual-schedule-series-first-then/

- Autism Parenting Magazine. (n.d.). Autism support groups: The ultimate guide. Retrieved July 19, 2025, from https://www.autismparentingmagazine.com/autism-support-groups-for-parents-families-children/

- Autism Parenting Magazine. (n.d.). Assistive communication devices for children with autism. Retrieved July 19, 2025, from https://www.autismparentingmagazine.com/assistive-technology-autism/

- Autism Research Institute. (2015). Brothers, sisters, and autism [PDF]. Retrieved July 19, 2025, from https://researchautism.org/wp-content/uploads/2016/04/OAR_SiblingResource_Parents_2015.pdf

- AutismSpeaks. (n.d.-a). ATN/AIR-P visual supports and autism [Toolkit]. Retrieved July 19, 2025, from https://www.autismspeaks.org/tool-kit/atnair-p-visual-supports-and-autism

- AutismSpeaks. (n.d.-b). Advocacy toolkit. Retrieved July 19, 2025, from https://www.autismspeaks.org/tool-kit/advocacy-tool-kit

- AutismSpeaks. (n.d.-c). Finding your community. Retrieved July 19, 2025, from https://www.autismspeaks.org/finding-your-community

- AutismSpeaks. (n.d.-d). Guide to individualized education programs (IEP). Retrieved July 19, 2025, from https://www.autismspeaks.org/tool-kit/guide-individualized-education-programs-iep

- AutismSpeaks. (n.d.-e). Life skills for autism. Retrieved July 19, 2025, from https://www.autismspeaks.org/life-skills-for-autism

- AutismSpeaks. (n.d.-f). M-CHAT-R (Modified checklist for autism in toddlers). Retrieved July 19, 2025, from https://www.autismspeaks.org/screen-your-child

- AutismSpeaks. (n.d.-g). Teaching your child self-advocacy. Retrieved July 19, 2025, from https://www.autismspeaks.org/tool-kit-excerpt/teaching-autism-self-advocacy

- AIDE Canada. (n.d.). Sensory processing differences toolkit. Retrieved July 19, 2025, from https://aidecanada.ca/resources/learn/sensory-regulation/sensory-processing-differences-toolkit

- AZA United. (2023, November). Aided language stimulation. Retrieved July 19, 2025, from https://azaunited.org/blog/modeling-language-without-expecting-a-response

- AZA United. (n.d.). A guide to self-care for parents of children with autism. Retrieved July 19, 2025, from https://azaunited.org/blog/self-care-for-parents-of-children-with-autism

- Carol Gray Social Stories. (n.d.). Social story sampler. Retrieved July 19, 2025, from https://carolgraysocialstories.com/social-stories/social-story-sampler/

- Cleveland Clinic Health Essentials. (n.d.). Debunking 8 autism myths and misconceptions. Retrieved July 19, 2025, from https://health.clevelandclinic.org/autism-myths-and-misconceptions

- Cleveland Clinic Health Essentials. (n.d.). Play therapy in children with autism: Its role, implications... Retrieved July 19, 2025, from https://www.ncbi.nlm.nih.gov/articles/PMC9850869/

- Logan, K., Iacono, T., et al. (2012). Increasing verbal responsiveness in parents of children with autism spectrum disorders. *Journal of Positive Behavior Interventions*, 14(4), 242–250. Retrieved from https://www.ncbi.nlm.nih.gov/articles/PMC3389583/

- Logan, K., Iacono, T., et al. (2022). The efficacy of visual activity schedule intervention in children with autism spectrum disorder. *Journal of Autism and Developmental Disorders.* Retrieved from https://www.ncbi.nlm.nih.gov/articles/PMC8733412/

- Medicaid.gov. (n.d.). Autism services. Retrieved July 19, 2025, from https://www.medicaid.gov/medicaid/benefits/autism-services

- Raising Children Network. (n.d.). Better sleep for autistic children (3–8 years): Tips. Retrieved July 19, 2025, from https://raisingchildren.net.au/autism/health-wellbeing/sleep/sleep-for-children-with-asd

- Sesame Workshop. (n.d.). Creating family traditions. Retrieved July 19, 2025, from https://sesameworkshop.org/resources/creating-family-traditions/

- Stages Learning. (n.d.). How to build an autism kit for on-the-go [Blog]. Retrieved July 19, 2025, from https://blog.stageslearning.com/blog/how-to-build-an-autism-kit-for-on-the-go

- Understood.org. (n.d.). Augmentative and alternative communication (AAC) [Replaced broken link]. Retrieved July 19, 2025, from https://www.asha.org/public/speech/disorders/aac/

www.ingramcontent.com/pod-product-compliance
Lightning Source LLC
Chambersburg PA
CBHW070800040426
42333CB00060B/1413